# GOD'S PLAN

## Two should not walk if they do not agree

*To Mrs Fellow*
*a person full of Compession.*

# Joan Parris

ISBN 978-1-68570-815-3 (paperback)
ISBN 978-1-68570-817-7 (hardcover)
ISBN 978-1-68570-816-0 (digital)

Christian Faith Publishing
832 Park Avenue
Meadville, PA 16335
www.christianfaithpublishing.com

Printed in the United States of America

thank the Lord God. You are the only true and dreadful God, yet you are the only loving and merciful God, and there is no one like you!

> The heavens declare the glory of God; and the firmament sheweth his handywork. Day unto day uttereth speech, and night unto night sheweth knowledge. There is no speech nor language, where their voice is not heard. Their line is gone out through all the earth, and their words to the end of the world. In them hath he set a tabernacle for the sun. (Psalm 19:1–4)

My hiding place, Emanuel—alpha and omega, the beginning and the end—I am not my own but thine, oh Lord!

Every tree that my heavenly Father did not plant in my life is rooted up in the name of Jesus!

My mother, Eunice, be strong and be of good courage. The Lord is with thee!

My beloved husband, Brian, as an anchor of provocation to pushing and propelling me very hard to get to know God's love deeper and show me how much God cares for me and God's protection from every storm in my friends' and family's lives!

God, reward Monique, Anashia, and Rochanda. You are more than a concour in Christ Jesus!

My daughter, Sisa, you are a daughter of Zion. Let no one tell you otherwise, my dear!

My granddaughter, Meilani, you are endowed with knowledge and wisdom!

Vanessa, may God open each door very wide before you.

All other grandchildren to come, the knowledge and wisdom become your potion in Jesus's name.

This book is dedicated to those who are seeking a deeper revelation from God and are in relationships that is a testament to your growth in Christ Jesus!

I have tasted and seen that the Lord is good! I have tasted the goodness of the Lord!

—Joan Parris

Written as remnant child and a piece written by my youngest daughter Rochanda as RAR, sharing her journey where she is coming from!

# CHAPTER 1

Two should not walk if they do not agree.

Prophets told me on different occasions that they had a word for me from God! I took that word for years seriously but didn't know that it would continue to follow me throughout my life! I know that God saves his anointed servants. I took the word of God, and later on, it started to manifest itself in me in the flesh. First it was a spiritual word that took place in my life. But the moment that I grabbed it in the spirit and took hold of it, it started to do me good.

I heard from God myself one day, years after that word was spoken to me, that as God was with Joshua, so he is with me! When the Lord reminded me sometime in June 2021 that as I was with Joshua, so I was with you. And the audio was very clear!

I know people who dig grave for other people are buried in the same grave that they dug themselves!

God has us in the palms of his hands that he looks at us continually! Do you know what is continually? He never takes his eyes off of us!

Or if you prefer to use any other quotes from these that are found below in the dictionary!

- always
- consistently
- constantly
- endlessly
- ever

+ evermore
+ forever
+ incessantly

You know my sitting down and my rising up;
You understand my thought afar off.
You comprehend my path and my lying down,
And are acquainted with all my ways.
For there is not a word on my tongue,
But behold, O Lord, You know it altogether.
You have hedged me behind and before,
And laid Your hand upon me.
Such knowledge is too wonderful for me;
It is high, I cannot attain it.
Where can I go from Your Spirit?
Or where can I flee from Your presence?
If I ascend into heaven, You are there;
If I make my bed in hell, behold, You are there.
If I take the wings of the morning,
And dwell in the uttermost parts of the sea,
Even there Your hand shall lead me,
And Your right hand shall hold me.
If I say, "Surely the darkness shall fall on me,"
Even the night shall be light about me;
Indeed, the darkness shall not hide from You,
But the night shines as the day;
The darkness and the light are both alike to You.
For You formed my inward parts;
You covered me in my mother's womb.
I will praise You, for I am fearfully and wonder-
fully made;
Marvelous are Your works,
And that my soul knows very well.
My frame was not hidden from You,
When I was made in secret,

And skillfully wrought in the lowest parts of the
earth.
Your eyes saw my substance, being yet unformed.
And in Your book they all were written,
The days fashioned for me,
When as yet there were none of them. (Psalm
139:2-16)

I prefer the way God does things for me, and I have no doubt or
desire to look for answers anywhere else except in the word of God!

Now I know that the Lord saves his anointed;
he will answer him from his holy heaven
with the saving might of his right hand.
Some trust in chariots and some in horses,
but we trust in the name of the Lord our God.
They collapse and fall,
but we rise and stand upright.
Oh Lord, save the king!
May he answer us when we call. (Psalm 20:6–9)

My setback is my comeback for miracles.

Each time I go to work, I leave with my left foot swollen so big
that I often wonder what is going on in my workplace. I pray for half
an hour every Friday afternoon before I go in to work even though I
get out of service at three thirty every Friday.

I have found out that men in general are fickle minded, and there
is nothing they will not do when they see that someone is about to
move up into a position that they think belongs to them. I would
advise a person to be careful of who they target because someone that
is assigned by God is grounded and cannot be moved even when those
that are fighting them think that they have them in a corner.

# 2
## CHAPTER

God has given me something special!

Prayer is such a dangerous weapon I know when it is in the right person's hands. And when you have it in your hand, be careful of how you use it. It is like playing with fire and not thinking that you can be burned—and not only burned but badly burned! Prayers move mountains and even shift things that are in place to hinder you. I can remember some of the fights that came before me and did not stand.

There was one person that I work with who thinks that I am an ordinary person that he can constantly do crazy things with spiritually to see if they could move me from my job. I can tell you that even my own husband knows that I am from a different breed! He would be drinking and would start texting my phone things that were unimaginable, and I would look on it and knew that he was drunk and never answered the phone.

Just a few days ago, I knew that a shift took place, and he started to call me like the world was ending. But I knew that the moon was full, and the enemy's plans would not work with me, as I am a remnant child of God. I know how difficult it is to be normal in this day and age as the force of darkness is looming so strong that you can see it when some people are speaking to you or even just looking at you.

It is good to give thanks unto the Lord.

It is good to give thanks to the Lord, to sing
praises to your name, O Most High; to declare

4

your steadfast love in the morning, and your faith-fulness by night, to the music of the lute and the harp, to the melody of the lyre. (Psalm 92:1–3)

We ask you, brothers, to respect those who labor among you and are over you in the Lord and admonish you, and to esteem them very highly in love because of their work. Be at peace among yourselves. And we urge you, brothers, admonish the idle, encourage the fainthearted, help the weak, be patient with them all. See that no one repays anyone evil for evil, but always seek to do good to one another and to everyone. Rejoice always, pray without ceasing, give thanks in all circumstances; for this is the will of God in Christ Jesus for you. Do not quench the Spirit. Do not despise proph-ecies, but test everything; hold fast what is good. Abstain from every form of evil. Now may the God of peace himself sanctify you completely, and may your whole spirit and soul and body be kept blameless at the coming of our Lord Jesus Christ. The one who calls you is faithful, and he will do it. (1 Thessalonians: 5:12–24)

For this reason I remind you to fan into flame the gift of God, which is in you through the laying on of my hands, for God gave us a spirit not of fear but of power and love and self-control. Therefore do not be ashamed of the testimony about our Lord, nor of me his prisoner, but share in suffering for the gospel by the power of God, who saved us and called us to a holy calling, not because of our works but because of his own pur-pose and grace, which he gave us in Christ Jesus before the ages began, and which now has been manifested through the appearing of our Savior

Christ Jesus, who abolished death and brought life
and immortality to light through the gospel, for
which I was appointed a preacher and apostle and
teacher, which is why I suffer as I do. (2 Timothy
1:6–12)

I was praising God—and I mean praising God—because I had
to face someone that was possessed, and it took me so many years to
deal with this demon that I was so intimidated! I know that something
changed when I would not speak or say a word when people
were quarreling, and I would be so quiet, and they were talking to me,
but I was talking to the Lord! When I walked in, he got up, and the
first word that came out of the mouth was a curse word. I stretched my
right hand out, and I said, "You foul spirit, the blood of Jesus is against
you. I commanded you out of that body in the name of Jesus Christ of
Nazareth." And I don't know what happened, but he shut up and sat
down on the couch and said not another word. I just spoke in tongues,
and then I walked away! I went to the restroom and took my shower.
After I was finished with my shower, I went to bed and slept!

I was sound asleep, and I heard the phone ringing. A little discombobulated,
I turned around and found the phone on the bedside
table.

"Hello! Hey, Mom."

"All night, Tom was texting me, and now I got so much disturbing
texts from him. I am calling to see what happened."

I said, "Oh, that. The Holy Spirit took care of him, and I am
sleeping."

Everyone that the Lord anoints is, for a reason, to destroy every
yoke of the enemies. I just remember Jesus and what it felt like to go
to sleep after dealing with that demon as Jesus fell asleep in the boat
when the waves were tossing the boat to and fro!

On that day, when evening had come, he said
to them, "Let us go across to the other side." And
leaving the crowd, they took him with them in the
boat, just as he was. And other boats were with

him. And a great windstorm arose, and the waves were breaking into the boat, so that the boat was already filling. But he was in the stern, asleep on the cushion. And they woke him and said to him, "Teacher, do you not care that we are perishing?" And he awoke and rebuked the wind and said to the sea, "Peace! Be still!" And the wind ceased, and there was a great calm. He said to them, "Why are you so afraid? Have you still no faith?" And they were filled with great fear and said to one another, "Who then is this, that even the wind and the sea obey him?" (Mark 4:35–41)

# 3 CHAPTER

She would put so much spiritual things at the workplace, but she realized that nothing was happening to me.

I had a Jeep Cherokee last year that I loved it so much that I would not give it up for anything. One morning, I came out after leaving work to go home. I got in my jeep and started to drive home and headed on the highway. I just got on, and the jeep was going about fifty miles per hour. When I pressed on the break, the break would not go down! I could remember that break would go down and would not come up, but mine would not go down. I called, "Jesus, Jesus, Jeeeesssssus!" And when I called, I called him so loud that if you were on the opposite side, you would hear me. And he answered me; and the break went down. I was traumatized for a few hours after experiencing the safety of God's mercy in my life, not because of the brake not going down but because of how quickly God answered me and kept me from the tragedy of an accident.

> Thus saith the Lord the maker thereof, the Lord that formed it, to establish it; the Lord is his name; Call unto me, and I will answer thee, and show thee great and mighty things, which thou knowest not. (Jeremiah 33:2)

> They shall not labour in vain, nor bring forth for trouble; for they are the seed of the blessed of the Lord, and their offspring with them. And

it shall come to pass, that before they call, I will
answer; and while they are yet speaking, I will
hear. (Isaiah 65:23–24)

When God shows up, it is your turn to receive your sevenfold
that is coming back to you!

Every morning, going to work in the city was a challenge as I
would deal with the traffic, driving from Queens to Manhattan. In
the city, there is no parking. When I say there is no parking, I mean
that the parking is very bad for people that drive in because the oppo-
site-side parking is always full, and people are sitting in their cars for
hours, waiting for a parking space outside in the streets.

I always go to work early to find a parking as going back home
is very challenging in the evenings when everyone is running for the
train, and the crowd is too much to deal with after a hard day of work.
This is my take on it! There are many people that just love this type of
lifestyle, but I cannot deal with the crowd, so it is better for me to drive
my own car to work.

I would sit in my car outside, praising the Lord and just knowing
that something was not right. I would do extra prayer and worship
the Lord more for a longer time. I don't know what people are doing,
and I don't care to know how they want to live their life when they are
informed that God is alive and well as he was in the days of John the
Baptist, so he is now and the days of all the other prophets of old!

And it may be that I will remain, or even
spend the winter with you, that you may send me
on my journey, wherever I go. For I do not wish to
see you now on the way; but I hope to stay a while
with you, if the Lord permits. But I will tarry in
Ephesus until Pentecost. 9For a great and effective
door has opened to me, and there are many adver-
saries. (1 Corinthians 16:6–9)

If any man love not the Lord Jesus Christ, let him be Anathema Maranatha. (1 Corinthians 16:22)

"Assuredly, I say to you, among those born of women there has not risen one greater than John the Baptist; but he who is least in the kingdom of heaven is greater than he. And from the days of John the Baptist until now the kingdom of heaven suffers violence, and the violent take it by force. For all the prophets and the law prophesied until John. And if you are willing to receive it, he is Elijah who is to come. He who has ears to hear, let him hear! (Matthew 11:11–15)

I got a park very fast this morning and sat there for a while. After I had finished my praise and worship, I thanked God for everything and asked the Lord to send the angels to remove every plan of the enemies in Jesus's mighty name!

I got out of my truck and headed toward the building that I have been working in for three years. I got in the elevator; and the moment I got to the floor, I knew that something was wrong but could not put my fingers on it, so to speak!

Man who is born of woman Is of few days and full of trouble. He comes forth like a flower and fades away; He flees like a shadow and does not continue. And do You open Your eyes on such a one, And bring me to judgment with Yourself? Who can bring a clean thing out of an unclean? No one! (Job 14:1–4)

I rang the doorbell, and the door was open. And as I stepped inside, the girl ran out. I texted her to get the information on the patient, and I only received foul language. And even until this day, I don't know what that girl had seen around me. I have not seen or heard from that young girl again! I got another person to fill her position.

> The wicked flee when no one pursues, But the righteous are bold as a lion. Because of the transgression of a land, many are its princes; But by a man of understanding and knowledge Right will be prolonged. (Proverbs 28:1–2)

> Treasures of wickedness profit nothing: but righteousness delivereth from death. The Lord will not suffer the soul of the righteous to famish: but he casteth away the substance of the wicked. (Proverbs 10:2–3)

> He that walketh uprightly walketh surely: but he that perverteth his ways shall be known. He that winketh with the eye causeth sorrow: but a prating fool shall fall. The mouth of a righteous man is a well of life: but violence covereth the mouth of the wicked. Hatred stirreth up strifes: but love covereth all sins. In the lips of him that hath understanding wisdom is found: but a rod is for the back of him that is void of understanding. (Proverbs 10:9)

# 4
## CHAPTER

**B**ut I know that the angels of the Lord surround them that fear him!

This poor man called out, and the Lord heard him; He saved him from all his troubles. The angel of the Lord encamps around those who fear Him, and he delivers them. Taste and see that the Lord is good; blessed is the man who takes refuge in Him! (Psalm 34:6–8)

In the multitude of words there wanteth not sin: but he that refraineth his lips is wise. The tongue of the just is as choice silver: the heart of the wicked is little worth. The lips of the righteous feed many: but fools die for want of wisdom. The blessing of the Lord, it maketh rich, and he addeth no sorrow with it. (Proverbs 10:19–22)

# 5
## CHAPTER

I came home after a long day and sat down at the dining table, eating my dinner, when I heard gunfire outside of my house! This was the first time in my life I had heard shots fired so close to where I live! I was talking to my husband, and all I could see was that he had thrown himself on the floor, as he was a military and police officer who retired from the United States. I threw myself on the floor and remembered my daughter was upstairs. I kept shouting to her to "duck, baby, duck, baby, duck!" All I heard from my husband was "be quiet!"

I was quiet until we heard that the sirens of police cars were all over outside. So we got up and started to peek through the window, looking where the shooting occurred! As we were looking out from our upstairs living room, we could see that most of the cars and vehicles were damaged from the top of the streets to the bottom where our vehicle was!

I said, "I know that my SUV is protected" as everyone came running to assess their own damages. I hadn't seen mine, but I knew that what God said to me stood! All the vehicles in front and behind my SUV were damaged, even on the opposite side of the road!

People were driving erratically to get away from the gunshots and the gunmen! I went to sleep as if nothing happened in my neighborhood. And late in the morning the next day, I decided to look at my SUV. And when I saw it, I began to sing praises to God and thanked God for his goodness because not even a scratch was on my vehicle!

Jehovah saw and heard our prayers!

I know that the expectations of the wicked in my life will not be met!

My trust is in the Lord as the word of God tells me that a horse is a vain thing for safety! All my reliance is in the true and living God!

# 6
## CHAPTER

was thinking of where I was at the present moment in my life. I heard the whisper of a small voice of God in my ears, "As I was with Joshua, so I am with you!"

As the time when the Jews got relief from their enemies, and as the month when their sorrow was turned into joy and their mourning into a day of celebration. He wrote them to observe the days as days of feasting and joy and giving presents of food to one another and gifts to the poor.

So the Jews agreed to continue the celebration they had begun, doing what Mordecai had written to them. For Haman son of Hammedatha, the Agagite, the enemy of all the Jews, had plotted against the Jews to destroy them and had cast the pur (that is, the lot) for their ruin and destruction. But when the plot came to the king's attention, he issued written orders that the evil scheme Haman had devised against the Jews should come back onto his own head, and that he and his sons should be impaled on poles. (Therefore these days were called Purim, from the word pur.) Because of everything written in this letter and because of what they had seen and what had happened to them, the Jews took it on themselves to establish the custom that they and their descendants and all who join them should without fail observe these two days every year, in the way prescribed and at the time appointed. (Esther 9:22–27)

And I commanded Joshua at that time, saying, Thine eyes have seen all that the Lord your God hath done unto these two kings: so shall the Lord do unto all the kingdoms whither thou passest.

Ye shall not fear them: for the Lord your God he shall fight for you.

And I besought the Lord at that time, saying,

O Lord God, thou hast begun to shew thy servant thy greatness, and thy mighty hand: for what God is there in heaven or in earth, that can do according to thy works, and according to thy might?

I pray thee, let me go over, and see the good land that is beyond Jordan, that goodly mountain, and Lebanon.

But the Lord was wroth with me for your sakes, and would not hear me: and the Lord said unto me, Let it suffice thee; speak no more unto me of this matter.

Get thee up into the top of Pisgah, and lift up thine eyes westward, and northward, and southward, and eastward, and behold it with thine eyes: for thou shalt not go over this Jordan.

But charge Joshua, and encourage him, and strengthen him: for he shall go over before this people, and he shall cause them to inherit the land which thou shalt see.

So we abode in the valley over against Bethpeor. (Deuteronomy 3)

I call heaven and earth to witness against you this day, that ye shall soon utterly perish from off the land whereunto ye go over Jordan to possess it; ye shall not prolong your days upon it, but shall utterly be destroyed.

And the Lord shall scatter you among the nations, and ye shall be left few in number among the heathen, whither the Lord shall lead you.

And there ye shall serve gods, the work of men's hands, wood and stone, which neither see, nor hear, nor eat, nor smell.

But if from thence thou shalt seek the Lord thy God, thou shalt find him, if thou seek him with all thy heart and with all thy soul.

When thou art in tribulation, and all these things are come upon thee, even in the latter days, if thou turn to the Lord thy God, and shalt be obedient unto his voice;

(For the Lord thy God is a merciful God;) he will not forsake thee, neither destroy thee, nor forget the covenant of thy fathers which he sware unto them.

For ask now of the days that are past, which were before thee, since the day that God created man upon the earth, and ask from the one side of heaven unto the other, whether there hath been any such thing as this great thing is, or hath been heard like it? (Deuteronomy 4)

# CHAPTER 7

*When a John Crow perched on a tree*

A treetop may seem to be a good place for the John Crow; but just be careful which treetop you try to perch on! There's fire on the top of my tree, so ask that your eyes be opened to see the tree where you want to stop and relax for a minute! I am not asking you; I am telling you that fire burns, and it burns in several degrees. When you check out the degrees, there are first-degree, second-degree, and third-degree burns!

The words of God are a consuming fire!

> Be careful not to forget the covenant of the Lord your God that he made with you; do not make for yourselves an idol in the form of anything the Lord your God has forbidden. For the Lord your God is a consuming fire, a jealous God. (Deuteronomy 4:23–24)

# 8
## CHAPTER

*Grateful and ungrateful*

I have been to many places. I have traveled many roads that are physical, roads that are spiritual that cannot be uttered or understood by just looking from afar, roads that elevate you, and the other roads that demolish you and help many people whom I thought were the perfect candidates that were somewhat foolish and selfish on my behalf! One of the things that are sure is that God is, and was, and is always with me.

There are times in our lives when you can sit down and reminisce on the favor of God in your own life, and I can do the same thing in my life. But we may not get the same results as we're all different in various ways! The things that I am grateful for are not always the same things others are grateful for! When I realized that I was placed in a position where I could be an asset to others or a hindrance, I prayed fervently about it that God would use me for his glory. I was not thinking. But even though I would like to be used by God, I didn't imagine that it was in this way.

I had spoken about home care in my first book, but I didn't elaborate on the details of the story on the way God worked for me to the maximum! At one point, I was just jumping from a regular paycheck to a company of half a million dollars a year! I was uncontrollable at that time even in God, taking vacation here and there, not knowing that I should have sat down and revered God! The problem was not that I was not giving into God ministries; the problem was that I was not consulting God! That would make an ordinary person go crazy, withered in God or out of God! God knows our best, and he knows our worst. I helped many people of all calibers, even peoples who were equipped with the ability to hire me instead of me hiring them. There was always one who would return to give thanks for the little things that were an impact in their life and would return to thank you when they had achieved their desired success and goals that they were looking for in their own life!

I can remember the first time I saw the man of God in South Africa; the people who were there, getting so much healing; and people who were prophetic under the anointed servants of God. At that moment, I thought to myself that I must meet with that man. This was only going on in my head, and I would start to plan my very meeting and what I would like to happen for me.

I couldn't pack a suitcase from my home because I was working, and I didn't get any time off because of how I had set up my work schedule. So now, everything had become complicated, not only that, but it was a secret. I was working it out in my head because I couldn't mention it to my husband! In my head, I was trying to figure out this travel, what I was going to do about it, and I didn't know how I was getting out of this one because I just wanted to go inside the house and not have to explain what I am doing or where I was going to because I plan to have a successful mission to leave for my next journey.

How was I going to get all these arrangements together without the whole world deciding for me? Everyone else always tried to tell me what to do, when to do it, and how to do it. I took a garage bag and put some clothes in the bag, and it looked as if I was taking the garbage out, but I took the bag to my SUV! I did not give anyone around me a clue on what was going on, but it appeared as if those were clothes that I was going to give away!

I drove to a store and bought a new suitcase, and I put the clothes from the bag into the suitcase, then I put the suitcase in the back of my SUV.

I went to work and called the airlines until I found a ticket to travel to South Africa. The next day, I said that I have an emergency, and this one could not wait. They were not happy with the sudden change, but they couldn't stop me as this emergency was with God and not with men! I got my flight to South Africa that day, only telling my children about it on the day that I was waiting to head off to get on the flight. My children are my keepers. They know my every move in anything I do. My husband has no interested in whatever I do. I had never been so relieved in my life before that time because I didn't have to tell a lie about me heading to another country

# 9
# CHAPTER

P eople always cry out about how life is complicated. Wait until they encounter the real life of other people!

That was all I needed to pivot myself forward to continue as the brilliancy of my daughters worked out perfectly. I came back full of resilience and reassurance with my head full with the great grace of God and excitement. For some reason, I couldn't contain all this excitement in my head.

I started sharing the experience I encountered in South Africa and the open vision I saw when I was heading back home on the plane. It was so real that I almost didn't want to believe that this was something I'd seen in the spirit. The moment I saw how much was given out to those people who were there, I was also rejoicing with them for their breakthrough!

# 10
## CHAPTER

*Grateful*

Some drank from the well of course and went on to start their own ministries! Some remained until now! I am one of those persons who came and never forgot about the burden that I had carried with me and never gave up on the idea that God is the same yesterday, today, and forever!

Jesus had similar encounters daily!

The problem with the ungrateful people is that they never take time to think about where they are coming from! It is like burning the bridge that takes them over passed the alligator under the bridge then burn it because there is no need to think about coming back over to that side of the bridge! I had come across a great number because of the amount of responsibility that was given to me! I had given jobs to people who were not grateful but stated that they were! Those people were the ones that turned around and took the very jobs that I paid them for, even talked about me with the same person I gave them to render services to, who feel it knows it!"

I can say now, may God punish the devil today in the name of Jesus Christ of Nazareth, Son of the living God!

Ungrateful people—those are persons who have no clue what the favor of God is, what God brings into their own life when they have met with the right persons! I dare to say that the same ungrateful persons who do these things can walk away from you today with no remorse!

I have seen so much of these things happen daily, and this only shows the reflection of their true colors. Are there characters in such person?

I dare not look for answers because we are all God's own handmade, and we are not call to make any harsh decisions about another person even though we would like to see each and every one of us who are in God follow the ordinance of God as Jesus walks on this earth before us!

One person asked me to give them a review and how I felt about the man of God! I began by saying, "The fact that I was there, and you were there, you didn't see me, but I saw you. When you had the opportunity that the man of God called you and let them give you a microphone to prophesy, and it was so real that I could feel the burden lifted from other people like myself, I couldn't see your heart beating, but I could imagine how many beats per second that it skipped in that very moment. You said, 'Daddy, I'm your number two!' When the anointing was strongly in the auditorium and praise and worship filled the place to honor the anointing of God in the house of God, the same ungrateful person that was called to prophesy burst into such beautiful songs singing, 'We're in your presence. Let it reign.' Could you remember that very moment?"

"I asked this ungrateful person by text when you were drinking from the anointing that day, 'It was very sweet, wasn't it?'" Then I asked the question that derailed every diabolic devil: "Was it good then? So why is it bitter now? Were you a part of the one third of the angels that was cast down with Satan? I don't know what could Satan have then, and I don't care to know now! My grandmother told me that dog that eats at two yards is no good! Why would you just bite the hands that feed you?" He deleted me!

"When we study the Bible, it tells us that leprosy starts on the inside then work itself on the outside! Is there leprosy on your inside working itself out? please go show yourself to the priest?

Ten lepers were cleansed; only one returned.

Now it happened as He went to Jerusalem
that He passed through the midst of Samaria and

Galilee. Then as He entered a certain village, there met Him ten men who were lepers, who stood afar off. And they lifted up their voices and said, "Jesus, Master, have mercy on us!"

So when He saw them, He said to them, "Go, show yourselves to the priests." And so it was that as they went, they were cleansed.

And one of them, when he saw that he was healed, returned, and with a loud voice glorified God, and fell down on his face at His feet, giving Him thanks. And he was a Samaritan.

So Jesus answered and said, "Were there not ten cleansed? But where are the nine? Were there not any found who returned to give glory to God except this foreigner?" And He said to him, "Arise, go your way. Your faith has made you well." (Luke 17)

And whatsoever ye do in word or deed, do all in the name of the Lord Jesus, giving thanks to God and the Father by him. (Colossians 3:17)

O give thanks unto the Lord; for he is good: for his mercy endureth for ever. (Psalm 136:1)

Cease not to give thanks for you, making mention of you in my prayers. (Ephesians 1:16)

Every good gift and every perfect gift is from above, and cometh down from the Father of lights, with whom is no variableness, neither shadow of turning. (James 1:17)

Wherefore we receiving a kingdom which cannot be moved, let us have grace, whereby we may serve God acceptably. (Hebrews 12:28)

And he brought the letter to the king of
Israel, saying, Now when this letter is come unto
thee, behold, I have therewith sent Naaman my
servant to thee, that thou mayest recover him of
his leprosy.

And it came to pass, when the king of Israel
had read the letter, that he rent his clothes, and
said, Am I God, to kill and to make alive, that this
man doth send unto me to recover a man of his
leprosy? wherefore consider, I pray you, and see
how he seeketh a quarrel against me.

And it was so, when Elisha the man of God
had heard that the king of Israel had rent his
clothes, that he sent to the king, saying, Wherefore
hast thou rent thy clothes? let him come now to
me, and he shall know that there is a prophet in
Israel.

So Naaman came with his horses and with
his chariot, and stood at the door of the house of
Elisha.

And Elisha sent a messenger unto him, saying, Go and wash in Jordan seven times, and thy
flesh shall come again to thee, and thou shalt be
clean.

But Naaman was wroth, and went away, and
said, Behold, I thought, He will surely come out
to me, and stand, and call on the name of the Lord
his God, and strike his hand over the place, and
recover the leper.

Are not Abana and Pharpar, rivers of
Damascus, better than all the waters of Israel?
may I not wash in them, and be clean? So he
turned and went away in a rage.

And his servants came near, and spake unto
him, and said, My father, if the prophet had bid
thee do some great thing, wouldest thou not have

done it? how much rather then, when he saith to thee, Wash, and be clean?

Then went he down, and dipped himself seven times in Jordan, according to the saying of the man of God: and his flesh came again like unto the flesh of a little child, and he was clean.

And he returned to the man of God, he and all his company, and came, and stood before him: and he said, Behold, now I know that there is no God in all the earth, but in Israel: now therefore, I pray thee, take a blessing of thy servant.

But he said, As the Lord liveth, before whom I stand, I will receive none. And he urged him to take it; but he refused.

And Naaman said, Shall there not then, I pray thee, be given to thy servant two mules' burden of earth? for thy servant will henceforth offer neither burnt offering nor sacrifice unto other gods, but unto the Lord.

In this thing the Lord pardon thy servant, that when my master goeth into the house of Rimmon to worship there, and he leaneth on my hand, and I bow myself in the house of Rimmon: when I bow down myself in the house of Rimmon, the Lord pardon thy servant in this thing.

And he said unto him, Go in peace. So he departed from him a little way.

But Gehazi, the servant of Elisha the man of God, said, Behold, my master hath spared Naaman this Syrian, in not receiving at his hands that which he brought: but, as the Lord liveth, I will run after him, and take somewhat of him.

So Gehazi followed after Naaman. And when Naaman saw him running after him, he lighted down from the chariot to meet him, and said, Is all well?

And he said, All is well. My master hath sent me, saying, Behold, even now there be come to me from mount Ephraim two young men of the sons of the prophets: give them, I pray thee, a talent of silver, and two changes of garments.

And Naaman said, Be content, take two talents. And he urged him, and bound two talents of silver in two bags, with two changes of garments, and laid them upon two of his servants; and they bare them before him.

And when he came to the tower, he took them from their hand, and bestowed them in the house: and he let the men go, and they departed.

But he went in, and stood before his master. And Elisha said unto him, Whence comest thou, Gehazi? And he said, Thy servant went no whither.

And he said unto him, Went not mine heart with thee, when the man turned again from his chariot to meet thee? Is it a time to receive money, and to receive garments, and oliveyards, and vineyards, and sheep, and oxen, and menservants, and maidservants?

The leprosy therefore of Naaman shall cleave unto thee, and unto thy seed for ever. And he went out from his presence a leper as white as snow. (2 Kings 5)

# 11
## CHAPTER

*I have learned*

Thank God that he is not like man that built you up for a failure. You can see how a lot of people started to prosper in their business with some companies, and they were so settled in their successes, and one morning they awakened by the IRS calling to destroy the years of hard work by auditing things that were already paid for years ago!

This just put you in a tailspin, then you would have no choice of what was going to happen because you had destroyed those files five years ago! Now they dropped you on your back, and your backbone was broken, not by the fall of a person pushing you down but from a spiritual fall that you could only get up by revelation and a strong prayer life! There were millions of reasons out there to help you, but because you called upon the Lord God to save you from drowning, he would pick you up from the fall. You would be restored!

# 12
## CHAPTER

*A father*

Bishop G. G. Cooper was so pleased to bless my manuscript for the first book that I had written! I called him to inform him months later that it was out, and it was on Amazon. When Bishop G.G. Cooper got the new about the manuscript his approach to the news was breathtaking.

Bishop said, "Let me get a copy that I can advertise it for you." I was so shocked! I was silence on my end because I was just bawling on the other side of the phone line, thanking God that he couldn't see me crying like that!

I dried up my tears and said, "Thank you for your love and being a father who is full of love and integrity!"

I was in service on the eighteenth of June, and in the end, I saw my father, Bishop Cooper, put my book up, explaining that it was the first book I had written and that I needed others to support me by buying it. "You tell me if there's anything that a father who is proud of his children wouldn't do for them? Jesus said, 'I and my father are one.' If you see me, you see the father!"

> I am the good shepherd, and know my sheep, and am known of mine. As the Father knoweth me, even so know I the Father: and I lay down my life for the sheep. And other sheep I have, which are not of this fold: them also I must bring, and

they shall hear my voice; and there shall be one fold, and one shepherd. Therefore doth my Father love me, because I lay down my life, that I might take it again. No man taketh it from me, but I lay it down of myself. I have power to lay it down, and I have power to take it again. This commandment have I received of my Father.

There was a division therefore again among the Jews for these sayings. And many of them said, He hath a devil, and is mad; why hear ye him? Others said, These are not the words of him that hath a devil. Can a devil open the eyes of the blind? (Matthews 14–21)

# 13
## CHAPTER

*Jehovah Sharma*

I see you everywhere, blessed Redeemer. Your glory fills the air. I know that you are my everlasting Father. You are the one who watches me. I put my confidence alone in you, Jehovah Sharma!

*A father*

> Father you are a loving God the only true and dreadful God! You are full of unfailing mercy! (John 10:28)

> That it may go well with you and that you may enjoy long life on the earth. Ephesians 6:1

Fathers, do not exasperate your children. Instead, bring them up in the training and instruction of the Lord. Slaves, obey your earthly masters with respect and fear and with sincerity of heart, just as you would obey Christ.

God has blessed me with two spiritual fathers. One plus one, it can never be two with me! How can it be when I don't even know what it's like with one as others have one father of their own? My two is one in God, so there's no jealousy as the body of Christ is one! I met both father in the same arena as they arrived on YouTube years apart. The first time I saw them, I just knew that they were my father's, and there was nothing else needed to be searching for! One of my fathers is living in Europe or South Africa. Wherever is home for him, it's well with me.

As Saul watched David going out to meet the Philistine, he said to Abner, commander of the army, "Abner, whose son is that young man?"

Abner replied, "As surely as you live, Your Majesty, I don't know."

The king said, "Find out whose son this young man is."

As soon as David returned from killing the Philistine, Abner took him and brought him before Saul, with David still holding the Philistine's head.

"Whose son are you, young man?" Saul asked him.

David said, "I am the son of your servant Jesse of Bethlehem." (1 Samuel 54–58)

# 14
## CHAPTER

B e careful whose son or daughter you are. Show me your father, and I will tell you whose child you are!

I met Pastor Alph Lukau in South Africa, and I was invited to dinner. The first time I was there, my thoughts were all over the place. After a little while, I realized that he was down to earth as if he had not a position at the top!

I honestly think that he is appointed for a time such as this. However, AMI is the foundation of his altar, of our Lord and Savior Jesus Christ, our God, for him to be so humble and adopt so many children of God. It tells of his strength in God and speak of his character!

I have been in the church a long time in my lifetime. And if you are not sensitive to the word of God and the calling of God, this is the true calling of my father's living in Jamaica, West Indies. The first time I physically met him, it was as if I knew him all my life. My heart adjusted to accept him.

I could see in him the fatherhood of a man that God has placed in the small island of Jamaica, a foundation to those who are seeking to get more of God that has no discrepancy in his ability to care for his children! I was one of those who've never had such grace in the flesh of a man that walked upright before and with God! I dare to say that Dr. Bishop G. G. Cooper is a father who can be reached for anything that's not contradictory in the Bible as he's walking totally in the word of God! Dr. Bishop G. G. Cooper and first lady, Carlene Cooper, is one of the true characters in the body of Christ that is an inspiration to others who are seeking more of God in this end-time!

Even though we're in a pandemic, and you can call it whatever it is to you, please just don't call it my name or anything close to it!

> King David rose to his feet and said: "Listen to me, my fellow Israelites, my people. I had it in my heart to build a house as a place of rest for the ark of the covenant of the Lord, for the footstool of our God, and I made plans to build it. But God said to me, 'You are not to build a house for my Name, because you are a warrior and have shed blood.'
>
> "Yet the Lord, the God of Israel, chose me from my whole family to be king over Israel forever. He chose Judah as leader, and from the tribe of Judah he chose my family, and from my father's sons he was pleased to make me king over all Israel. Of all my sons—and the Lord has given me many—he has chosen my son Solomon to sit on the throne of the kingdom of the Lord over Israel. He said to me: 'Solomon your son is the one who will build my house and my courts, for I have chosen him to be my son, and I will be his father. I will establish his kingdom forever if he is unswerving in carrying out my commands and laws, as is being done at this time. (1 Chronicles 28:2–7)

I can tell you that he's a father who is reachable. Even though he is high in authority and has a lot of responsible, he took time out for his children and picked up his phone when it rang!

There was never a time when you called him and he ever complained to you about a thing. I can tell you that this is the love of God that the Bible speaks about to you and I in his words.

One reference is that I called once in a while, and I was just blown away with the way the bishop answered with grace at all times.

And I gave unto them eternal life; and they shall never perish, neither shall any man pluck them out of my hand. My Father, which gave them me, is greater than all; and no man is able to pluck them out of my Father's hand. I and my Father are one.

Then the Jews took up stones again to stone him. Jesus answered them, Many good works have I shewed you from my Father; for which of those works do ye stone me? The Jews answered him, saying, For a good work we stone thee not; but for blasphemy; and because that thou, being a man, makest thyself God. Jesus answered them, Is it not written in your law, I said, Ye are gods? If he called them gods, unto whom the word of God came, and the scripture cannot be broken; Say ye of him, whom the Father hath sanctified, and sent into the world, Thou blasphemest; because I said, I am the Son of God? If I do not the works of my Father, believe me not. But if I do, though ye believe not me, believe the works: that ye may know, and believe, that the Father is in me, and I in him. Therefore they sought again to take him:

but he escaped out of their hand. (John 10:31)

The righteous man walks in his integrity; his children are blessed after him. (Proverbs 20:7)

# 15
## CHAPTER

*Don't lose sight.*

Satan's plan was to get the attention of the woman. When God made man, it was for us to live in the Garden of Eden and never be in wanted for anything at all. When Satan sees the plan of God in believers' lives how much they trust God, it rattled him as he was the highest angel in heaven that sang and ministered to God! He expired his time when he became very envious of the blessing of God. He, Satan, started to think on how he could have what God has! I can imagine how he sat down day after day and night after night to hash out a plan to see if he could dethrone God.

The Bible tells us that he has no intention of stopping even now. He tries everything that attach to the promise of God. Satan goes to and fro from heaven to earth to see if he could accuse us daily. When Satan was thrown out of heaven, he started a campaign that was just the beginning of the plan he had in mind because he is very intelligent. Do you want to know how intelligent Satan is?

Check the way he tempted Jesus when he went and followed Jesus after his fasting on the mountain.

At that time Jesus was led by the Spirit into the desert to be tempted by the devil. He fasted for forty days and forty nights and afterwards was hungry. The tempter approached and said to him, "If you are the Son of God, command that these stones become loaves of bread. Jesus answered, "It is written: 'Man shall not live on bread alone, but on every word that comes from the mouth of God.'"

Then the devil took him to the holy city and had him stand on the highest point of the temple. "If you are the Son of God," he said, "throw yourself down. For it is written:

"'He will command his angels concerning you, and they will lift you up in their hands, so that you will not strike your foot against a stone.'"

Jesus answered him, "It is also written: 'Do not put the Lord your God to the test.'"

Again, the devil took him to a very high mountain and showed him all the kingdoms of the world and their splendor. "All this I will give you," he said, "if you will bow down and worship me." (Matthew 4:1–11)

Don't lose sight of where you are going! When Satan sees that he can't get Jesus's attention, he starts to strategize how to get someone's attention.

He was hiding in the Garden of Eden somewhere, plotting to see what he could use.

# 16
## CHAPTER

*Jesus and the fig tree!*

When I went to South Africa, I was waiting on the prophet to speak a word in my life. When it didn't happen, I was not happy with the back and forth. However, I kept going back to see if I would get the word directly from him, but I didn't even realize that I was already drinking from the well! I was still looking forward for the man of God to locate me at some point whenever he is passing where I am sitting. I tell myself that I am the next person he will call every time I'm there in person.

Then the next time came and went, and then the next, but nothing happened! I woke up with this amazing realization that if only I could connect myself with the God of the man that was in the prophet and not the man in the flesh, I should receive what I was looking for!" I had met with the God in the man, and the God of the man was bigger and mightier and full of power than the man!

I'm basking in the presence of the God of man I can. tell you that the God of man is real as you have seen the man today. I have spoken to God, and he reminded me that there is no other God before him, or there will be none other after him! To those who are still waiting and seeking other gods, please let go and let God show you how he does mighty things; that will blow your mind.

Jesus was hungry and looking for something to eat when he came up to the fig tree, and I could imagine that he just lost it looking at the fig tree, and no fruit was there!

On the following day, when they came from Bethany, he was hungry. And seeing in the distance a fig tree in leaf, he went to see if he could find anything on it. When he came to it, he found nothing but leaves, for it was not the season for figs. And he said to it, "May no one ever eat fruit from you again." And his disciples heard it. (Mark 11:12–14)

And a man shall be as an hiding place from the wind, and a covert from the tempest; as rivers of water in a dry place, as the shadow of a great rock in a weary land. (Isaiah 32:2)

I said to myself that this was the first time I've heard that Jesus spoke to any trees in this manner!

And all the trees of the field shall know that I the Lord have brought down the high tree, have exalted the low tree, have dried up the green tree, and have made the dry tree to flourish: I the Lord have spoken and have done [it]. (Ezekiel 17:24)

# 17
## CHAPTER

*Elisha with Elijah—Elijah taken up to heaven*

When the Lord was about to take Elijah up to heaven in a whirlwind, Elijah and Elisha were on their way from Gilgal. Elijah said to Elisha, "Stay here; the Lord has sent me to Bethel."

But Elisha said, "As surely as the Lord lives and as you live, I will not leave you." So they went down to Bethel.

The company of the prophets at Bethel came out to Elisha and asked, "Do you know that the Lord is going to take your master from you today?"

"Yes, I know," Elisha replied, "so be quiet."

Then Elijah said to him, "Stay here, Elisha; the Lord has sent me to Jericho."

And he replied, "As surely as the Lord lives and as you live, I will not leave you." So they went to Jericho.

The company of the prophets at Jericho went up to Elisha and asked him, "Do you know that the Lord is going to take your master from you today?"

"Yes, I know," he replied, "so be quiet."

Then Elijah said to him, "Stay here; the Lord has sent me to the Jordan."

And he replied, "As surely as the Lord lives and as you live, I will not leave you." So the two of them walked on.

Fifty men from the company of the prophets went and stood at a distance, facing the place where Elijah and Elisha had stopped at the Jordan. Elijah took his cloak, rolled it up and struck the water with it. The water divided to the right and to the left, and the two of them crossed over on dry ground.

When they had crossed, Elijah said to Elisha, "Tell me, what can I do for you before I am taken from you?"

As they were walking along and talking together, suddenly a chariot of fire and horses of fire appeared and separated the two of them, and Elijah went up to heaven in a whirlwind. Elisha saw this and cried out, "My father! My father! The chariots and horsemen of Israel!" And Elisha saw him no more. Then he took hold of his garment and tore it in two.

Elisha then picked up Elijah's cloak that had fallen from him and went back and stood on the bank of the Jordan. He took the cloak that had fallen from Elijah and struck the water with it. "Where now is the Lord, the God of Elijah?" he asked. When he struck the water, it divided to the right and to the left, and he crossed over.

The company of the prophets from Jericho, who were watching, said, "The spirit of Elijah is resting on Elisha." And they went to meet him and bowed to the ground before him. "Look," they said, "we your servants have fifty able men. Let them go and look for your master. Perhaps the Spirit of the Lord has picked him up and set him down on some mountain or in some valley."

"No," Elisha replied, "do not send them."

But they persisted until he was too embarrassed to refuse. So he said, "Send them." And they
sent fifty men, who searched for three days but did
not find him. When they returned to Elisha, who
was staying in Jericho, he said to them, "Didn't I
tell you not to go?" (2 Kings 2)

Knowing that Elijah's assignment was in full progression with God
as Elisha knew that one day he would taste the goodness of God,
everywhere Elijah went, Elisha followed because there was something he wanted so bad he could touch it.

# 18
## CHAPTER

*Right and wrong*

I am so excited to hear that as I looked out the window overlooking the backyard, there's a Chinese maple tree that is very huge outstretched across the lawn! I see the cardinals, the blue jays, the morning dove, and the sparrows. There are some birds that I don't have a clue what they are, but I just love to see them and feed them in the mornings!

I am presenting to you real life titles of some persons, like the ones that are not known as no one has ever even thought of their names or titles. As nature presents itself before me, I could choose right or wrong, but I have decided to choose right.

Now I was there, doing my coffee, and a crazy thought came to my head to put some eggs on the stove to make some egg salads. I got the eggs out and put them in water and turned the stove on! Then another thought popped in my head, and when a person that I know came in, I started to share some great ideas and news with him. I sat down comfortably with no other thought but to talk about the goodness of God and what had been happening in my life with my mind only on Christ. While I was talking away about a lot of things, the person on the other end of the line became another person altogether!

The conversation went into a downward spiral, and then it became a little toxic to my ears as there were people who were in church but not in God! I hung up the phone and said to myself, "Oh, Lord, what was that"! Then I smelled that the water was dried, out and my eggs were burning! I ran into the kitchen and took the pot outside before the fire alarm went on and brought it outside and left it to cool off before putting water in the pot! I said to myself again, "Oh, Lord God, can somebody burn eggs!" I started laughing. "Oh, Lord, I just did it!" The truth is that right and wrong cannot walk together. There are millions of things out there that are right and millions of things that are wrong; chose the one that is right for you!

> And let the peace of God rule in your hearts, to the which also ye are called in one body; and be ye thankful. (Colossians 3:15)

> And we know that all things work together for good to them that love God, to them who are the called according to his purpose. (Romans 8:28)

> O give thanks unto the Lord, for he is good: for his mercy endureth for ever. (Psalm 107:1)

> Whoso offereth praise glorifieth me: and to him that ordereth his conversation aright will I shew the salvation of God. (Psalm 50:23)

> Giving thanks always for all things unto God and the Father in the name of our Lord Jesus Christ. (Ephesians 5:20)

# 19

## CHAPTER

*Fruit basket*

Everyone has a fruit basket, weather it belongs to you or you borrowed it! My fruit basket is full with so many different types of fruits and vegetables that I myself don't know the nature of its existence. Some are good fruits and vegetables, but some are bad ones, depending upon the days that you decide to pick a fruit or vegetable out of it!

> For husbands, this means love your wives, just as Christ loved the church. (Ephesians 5:25)

> Therefore a man shall leave his father and his mother and hold fast to his wife, and they shall become one flesh. (Genesis 2:24)

> Likewise, husbands, live with your wives in an understanding way, showing honor to the woman as the weaker vessel since they are heirs with you of the grace of life so that your prayers may not be hindered. (1 Peter 3:7)

> Husbands, love your wives and do not be harsh with them. (Colossians 3:19)

Wives, submit yourselves to your own husbands as you do to the Lord. For the husband is the head of the wife as Christ is the head of the church, his body, of which he is the Savior. Now as the church submits to Christ, so also wives should submit to their husbands in everything. (Ephesians 5:22–33)

Therefore be imitators of God, as beloved children. And walk in love, as Christ loved us and gave himself up for us, a fragrant offering and sacrifice to God. But sexual immorality and all impurity or covetousness must not even be named among you, as is proper among saints.

Let there be no filthiness nor foolish talk nor crude joking, which are out of place, but instead let there be thanksgiving. For you may be sure of this, that everyone who is sexually immoral or impure, or who is covetous (that is, an idolater), has no inheritance in the kingdom of Christ and God. (Ephesians 5:1–33)

# 20
# CHAPTER

*Tanted*

When my basket or anyone's basket is touched or has fruits that are not good to enjoy, there is a change in everything in your home and life! Some drink strange water, and the water contaminates the whole basket as there will be foul things coming out of it!

Don't mind that as, in other people's baskets, there's other fruits that appeared to be burdened to the basket. Now that, that basket some years to get its balance, and get back to a stage where it is recognized as that basket is not a basket that can be trusted to eat fruit or vegetables from again!

Peter and the other disciples were in the boat, and everything was just fine until a storm came and disrupted them!

Now he looked out and saw someone in the distance, and the first thing that came to them was fear because they thought that it was a ghost. But after looking well, their perceptions changed. They recognized that it was Jesus. "Oh, Lord, look, it's Jesus. I'm very excited!" When you are in a boat, please continue to look for Jesus! "Peter called out to Jesus and said, "Jesus, if it's you, bid me to come to you." That is a faith carrier!

Have you weighed the possibility of you being Peter after seeing how the ocean was very rough?

And the boat was already a considerable distance from land, buffeted by the waves because the wind was against it.

Shortly before dawn Jesus went out to them, walking on the lake. When the disciples saw him walking on the lake, they were terrified. "It's a ghost," they said, and cried out in fear.

But Jesus immediately said to them: "Take courage! It is I. Don't be afraid."

"Lord, if it's you," Peter replied, "tell me to come to you on the water."

"Come," he said.

Then Peter got down out of the boat, walked on the water and came toward Jesus. But when he saw the wind, he was afraid and, beginning to sink, cried out, "Lord, save me!"

Immediately Jesus reached out his hand and caught him. "You of little faith," he said, "why did you doubt?" (Matthew 14–24)

As you take your eyes away from Jesus, there's always something that will wake you up and remind you that Jesus is in front of you!

I encourage you today; keep your eyes on Jesus. You will never sink!

"Some people's preferences are literally making me dizzy as they're those who have made up their minds to go around and make it their assignment to contaminated other people's baskets and then wait for the basket to be thrown out into the garbage pile. This is where they would return to pick up that basket!

> Consume them in wrath, consume them, that they may not be: and let them know that God ruleth in Jacob unto the ends of the earth. Selah.
>
> And at evening let them return; and let them make a noise like a dog, and go round about the city.

Let them wander up and down for meat, and
grudge if they be not satisfied. (Psalm 59:15)

I think it's not a good thing as you and I deserve to have good fruits and vegetables to eat, but that will help us to get out of our comfort zone and check the fruits and vegetables daily in our basket! There are days when; you can smell some of your fruits that they are rotten, and when you check the bottom of the basket you realize that it's indeed rotten. I urged you to stay on top of your prayer life for your fruits baskets, and don't forget to check it often or one bad apple or banana will spoil the entire basket!"

For whosoever will save his life shall lose it;
but whosoever shall lose his life for my sake and
the gospel's, the same shall save it. For what shall it
profit a man, if he shall gain the whole world, and
lose his own soul? (Mark 8:34–38)

I know that when a person reads this, they will be wondering, why a fruit basket? I thought my fruit basket was the worst until I have been to different places and saw other people's own fruit baskets. I wouldn't exchange mine for anyone else's, not even for a day!

Have you ever weighed the good and bad fruits and vegetables in your fruit basket to see if there are more good ones than the rotten ones? If you don't get the revelations out of this, common sense cannot be taught!

If the Spirit of Christ dwells in you, truly the
thinking of your fleshly body is dead. Otherwise
its outcome would be sin. However the thinking
of the Spirit is life, because through that thinking
you do right.

If the Spirit of him who raised Jesus Christ
from the dead dwells in you, then he who raised
Christ from death will also give life to your dying

bodies. He will do this through his Spirit who dwells in you.

So brethren we are not obliged to the flesh to live in the fleshly mindset. In fact, if you do live in the way of the flesh you will die. But if you, by the Spirit, put to death the sinful deeds of your fleshly body, you will live. In fact, all who are led by the Spirit are sons and heirs of God. (Romans 8:10–14)

Jesus said, "Be faithful until death and I will give you the crown of life" (Revelation 2:10).

Paul wrote along similar lines... "I have fought the good fight, I have finished the course, I have kept the faith. Henceforth there is laid up for me the crown of righteousness which the Lord, the righteous Judge, will award me on that day, and not only to me but to all who have loved his appearing" (2 Timothy 4:7).

Sometimes Christians are required to die for their faith. For most of us, however, we are required only to maintain our faith until we die. This is not such a big thing to ask when the Lord has been so wonderful to us and when he helps us in every step of the way.

But every man is tempted, when he is drawn away of his own lust, and enticed.

Then when lust hath conceived, it bringeth forth sin: and sin, when it is finished, bringeth forth death. (James 1)

# 21
## CHAPTER

*The care/burden of God*

S on of Man, can these bones live? Yeah, Lord, you know as God moved the assignment of one prophet to another!

He asked me, "Son of man, can these bones live?"

I said, "Sovereign Lord, you alone know."

Then he said to me, "Prophesy to these bones and say to them, 'Dry bones, hear the word of the Lord! This is what the Sovereign Lord says to these bones: I will make breath[a] enter you, and you will come to life. I will attach tendons to you and make flesh come upon you and cover you with skin; I will put breath in you, and you will come to life. Then you will know that I am the Lord.'"

So I prophesied as I was commanded. And as I was prophesying, there was a noise, a rattling sound, and the bones came together, bone to bone. I looked, and tendons and flesh appeared on them and skin covered them, but there was no breath in them.

Then he said to me, "Prophesy to the breath; prophesy, son of man, and say to it, 'This is what the Sovereign Lord says: Come, breath, from the four winds and breathe into these slain, that they may live."' So I prophesied as he commanded me, and breath entered them; they came to life and stood up on their feet—a vast army.

Then he said to me: "Son of man, these bones are the people of Israel. They say, 'Our bones are dried up and our hope is gone; we are cut off.' Therefore prophesy and say to them: 'This is what the Sovereign Lord says: My people, I am going to open your graves and bring you up from them; I will bring you back to the land of Israel. Then you, my people, will know that I am the Lord, when I open your graves and bring you up from them. I will put my Spirit in you and you will live, and I will settle you in your own land. Then you will know that I the Lord have spoken, and I have done it, declares the Lord."' (Ezekiel 37:3–14)

I could imagine Moses when he saw the behavior of the people whom he left very good before he went up on the mountains to pray. When he returned, they were a different kind of people. They destroyed every valuable anointing that was bestowed upon them; during the time when Pharaoh's reign in Egypt how he had treated God's people badly, and God delivered them from Pharaoh's hands; as they left all their troubles behind in the Red Sea.

"Now, oh Lord! You tell me what to do with these people?"

He asked the Lord, "Why have you brought this trouble on your servant? What have I done to displease you that you put the burden of all these people on me? (Numbers 11:11)

Moses continued, "At that time I told you, 'You are too great a burden for me to carry all by myself." (Deuteronomy 1:9)

There is a great difference, of course, between man's repentance and God's repentance. Man's repentance involves turning from sin to God. But when the Bible speaks of God repenting, there is no thought of sin. Neither is there any hint of vacillation, as if God wavers in His purpose or changes His plans in response to man's doings. God is unchanging or immutable. His purpose has been fixed from eternity, and He will establish it (Isaiah 46:10; Ephesians 1:11).

He does not change His mind as man does (1 Samuel 15:29).

# 22
## CHAPTER

*Walking with God*

When the Lord said, "I will go before you and make every crooked way straight!"

When the Lord said I will go before you and make every crooked way straight!

I got a phone call one day, and I didn't recognize the number. I answered, "Praise the Lord!" The person on the other side introduced herself and explained how she got my number! We talked and work out a good plan to work at her home, and the fees I charged was high at that time, but she decided to pay me!

I was not even looking for a job at this point because I had just gotten a settlement of a sizable amount of money! However, I said, "God, did you do this and give me this job as I was not looking for one? I started working with this person a week later, and it was great as I was only doing five hours per day for four days. As time went by, the assignment began to extend, and I was glad at first because of the sizable amount of money on my check when I received it! Then the person who was covering the weekend quit, so they asked me to cover the weekend.

My first weekend was a plan of torture that no one serving the true and living God has any business doing it! I got to realize why the young lady quit! She was in turmoil on the weekends. I just came up with a good excuse and let them know that I would not be able to cover the weekend anymore, so they should find someone else!

They got someone else from an agency, but they kept changing them frequently, and they kept asking me, but I refused also because no one could sit down for a minute on the weekend, and this was the time when they wanted to run up and down the street from morning until evening. You were the one to push them in a wheelchair! When the day was over, you would be so burnt out from the sun and exhausted from walking!

I was very brave to continue the weekdays for a number of years. The next challenge came when the person who was working in the weekdays quit also, and I was left to covered the weekdays. When I asked her why she was quitting, she reminded me that the person was hypochondriac, and she could not deal with this situation anymore as this type of person's problem is medical (which means a person who is abnormally anxious about their health).

I came to realize that this was not only medical but spiritual also!

I was not this grounded in prayer because I couldn't get rid of those demons out of that house. When I was at the home in the night, my head was feeling heavy, had headaches, and no sleep!

I got a young lady to work for a few days per week as she was already working for my company for a couple years before now! I was not aware of this magnitude of evil before at a workplace. I was constantly fighting with the client for nothing, but there arose more where it was just problems, and I have been working there a few years now! One morning I was early, so I sat down in my vehicle and had another hour of devotion again. I prayed, then I came in to work. And as soon as I entered the room, the lady ran out! I didn't know what she was seeing around me, but I knew that it was not usual. I called her, and all I got from her was bad, foul languages.

The Bible said that the wicked run when no one is chasing them!

The wicked run when no one is chasing them, but an honest person is as brave as a lion.

As brave as a lion. When a nation sins, it will have one ruler after another. But a nation will be strong and endure when it has intelligent, sensible leaders. Someone in authority who oppresses poor people is like a driving rain that destroys the crops. (Proverbs 28:1–3)

I started praying dangerous prayers that started to shift things and splashed holy water around when I prayed in the night with a lot of warfare prayer! I was praying in a different room one day, and the next morning, the patient said to me that I came in the room and wet up everything and asked why I came to the room last night!

I was not in the room, and I didn't wet up anyone! I was telling a pastor what took place, and he told me that it was the holy water that I was splashing around inside the house that caught the demons in the night!

Now this was a problem that I was not looking for! Every week, this was still going on, and I became overwhelmed with this assignment, and I started to ask God what I had to do! I kept getting answers that I really didn't like, and now I was trying to hand over this assignment to someone else, but I can tell you that when something is given to you by God, you just can't run away from it because I tried, and it didn't work! The devil is a liar, and he tries to steal and destroy even my very thought!

I said to the Lord, "Lord, I am quitting, and it's you who gave me this assignment. I am giving up to two months. I cannot handle this anymore, and you always finish what you started because I am going on vacation now for three weeks. And when I come back to work, you work it out." On the weekend before I took my vacation, the next week, the patient ended up in the hospital!

The person who covered the weekend gave me the report, and I didn't want to deal with this situation now. My assignments became a little easier as I was not working anywhere else with the patient. I was praying that this assignment be passed from me like never before in my life!

There was never a time in my life that I had to pray that my work assignment should be passed from me because of the traffic of evil I encounter in the place. As I was praying one night before I leave work the next day, I clearly heard something like a frog in the other room where my assignment was! It was about two thirty in the morning. I heard the sound, and I couldn't even close my eyes.

Thank God it was Thursday. I knew that the following day, I would be going home! I went in later on in the morning, and I realized that my patient was not so well, and I offered to help in every way possible, then I got some tea and gave it to the patient.

The other person who covered the shift was there to take over the shift from me, and I gave the report. When I told her that the person was not doing well, she said, "Why did you not call me and tell me that the patient was sick, and I could stay home!"

I said to her, "Why would I do that? Who would I leave the patient with!"

She said that she didn't want to stay with the patient because she was afraid in the house! I encouraged her to pray and reminded her that God didn't give us a spirit of fear but of love, power, and a sound mind! This patient stayed in the hospital until she passed away!

Everyone who knew me said I must be saddened because the money was so good! I said, "I thank God for delivering me out of this assignment, and I didn't have to quit. You are talking about money!"

I am just opening your mind to the revelations about how Satan is cunning!

The Bible said that the wealth of the wicked is laid up for the just!

I am working at my job for years, and every time I come to that place, my feet swell up, and I can't even sleep in this place as hard as I try!

I was lying on the bed, and I was reading a scripture. And after that, I was listening to a song playing on YouTube when I felt the side of my head, and I felt a big ball, like a tennis ball, appeared on my head!

I took the Bible up, and I used my right hand and slapped the Bible on the side where the ball appeared and said, "Devil, eat the word of God! (Satan *nam di* word of God!) I command you to pluck up from the root in Jesus's name!" I felt the presence jumped off my head and left!

My eyes opened after a while to see the wickedness of someone doing their own wickedness! After I started praying dangerous prayers, things started shifting. I always knew that I had something in me that manifest itself when I pray because I tried my best to live right with God and always have a clean heart and hands! When I actually started seeing the manifestation in the flesh, it was more than awesome!

I came in, and the person who was present at work said something to me about rubbing her Buddha's belly, and I told her I only worship the true and living God! I walked away, and then she turned to me and asked me if I was a witch. I said, "No, I only serve the Lord God Almighty!"

She realized that every time she did things in the workplace, it affected her and not me. I came in one day, and she asked me to pray for her. She said, "You are the most religious person I have ever met!" I don't know what she was talking about as she was a Jewish person who knew about religion already!

I told her that I pray in the name of Jesus, and she said that it's all right! I knew her reason for asking for prayer! It was only last week that she had asked me to cover her shift at work. And when I was to be paid, she envied my paycheck. As she did that, the Holy Spirit let me ask her how much hours in a day because I was the person who covered the entire day!

Then the parables of the man who had the vineyard and hired men and ask them how much they charge for the day, but when the last man came and was later on in the day, but he gave him the same amount as the others. The next morning, I came in. She said to me, "You are 100 percent right!" I left her. And that weekend was the beginning of all her troubles because I prayed! I was listening to a sermon on YouTube, and I heard clearly that I would do terrible things. I was not sure if I heard what I was hearing! I stopped for a while, and then the Lord led me to a part in the Bible that showed me a scripture. God keeps on blessing me and showing me a lot of favors as it was written in the Bible about the husbandman that had the vineyard (Matt. 20:1–16). God keep on doing what he does best and the husbandman was very favorable to me, and showed me the same favor as was written in the word of God!

I started to explain to her about the parable Jesus spoke about.

Jesus tells the parable of the workers in the vineyard to further explain what the kingdom of God is like. A landowner goes out early in the morning and hires men, agreeing to pay them the daily rate—a silver coin for a day's work. When they too were given the standard daily wage, they began to grumble. They were angry because they had done a lot more work than those who had started later in the day (Matthew 20: 1–16).

> And he said, Behold, I make a covenant:
> before all thy people I will do marvels, such as have
> not been done in all the earth, nor in any nation:
> and all the people among which thou [art] shall
> see the work of the Lord: for it [is] a terrible thing
> that I will do with thee. (Exodus 34:10)

I called someone else. I was talking to them, and I said, "This can't be the Lord. It must be that woman's demons trying to let me think that way!"

I came in to work, and the lady car couldn't move. Something was wrong at her house. They were calling her to come to get it fixed, and now she needed a car to get home! I then offered to get an Uber for her to take her to the rental place for her to rent a car!

> I will go before thee, and make the crooked
> places straight; I will break in pieces the gates of
> brass, and cut in sunder the bars of iron. (Isaiah
> 45:2)

You would think that was enough, but no. Her troubles had just started! She was not able to come back to work until two weeks later! The money that she envied me for became her demise. The problem with this woman was too much! I followed her outside, and I put my hands up in surrender to the Lord God Almighty; and I started to pray. When I was finished with the prayer, she turned to me and said, "Oh, God, this is the most beautiful prayer I have ever heard." She showed me her hands and said, "Look at so much goosebumps, especially when you speak that different language!" I was praying in tongues, and the Holy Spirit showed up the trees were just swaying so hard, it couldn't be missed!

One week later, when she got to work on the first day of our forty days of fasting, I left work, and I was at home worshipping God!

I got a call the next day in the afternoon on Tuesday, on the second day of our fasting. I was not working until the weekend, and it was very strange for them to call me a day later after I just left work! I took the call, and they were asking me to come back to work, but I wanted to spend time with my family. As I was calling around to find someone to cover her shift, I couldn't find anyone to do the job! Even though I found people, they didn't want to go. But the assignment was mine. It was 4:00 p.m., and I was not thinking about any work for myself, much less anyone!

The problem arose into a more persistent matter that I had to go. I came in, and she was already heading out. I asked her if she couldn't stay until the next day, and she told me that she had some problems, and she didn't want to wait to deal with it. She left. Two weeks passed, and we spoke for the first week. And then the communication between us was ended. She had never answered our calls anymore. It's now four months, and I have been working both my assignments and hers! No one knows what happened to her, but I know that she is around because, yesterday, someone else said that she called them! God's word never fails me!

Who is your God? What is your God doing for you?

> Call unto Me, and I will answer thee, and show thee great and mighty things, which thou knowest not. (Jeremiah 33:3)

# 23

## CHAPTER

*The alignment of the mouth and the heart*

The heart is aligned with the mouth, and the words which come out of your mouth will either heal you or kill you.

> As a man thinks
> Do not overwork to be rich;
> Because of your own understanding, cease!
> Will you set your eyes on that which is not?
> For riches certainly make themselves wings;
> They fly away like an eagle toward heaven.
> Do not eat the bread of a[b] miser,
> Nor desire his delicacies;
> For as he thinks in his heart, so is he.
> "Eat and drink!" he says to you,
> But his heart is not with you.
> The morsel you have eaten, you will vomit up,
> And waste your pleasant words.
> Do not speak in the hearing of a fool,
> For he will despise the wisdom of your words.
> Out of the abundance (Proverbs 23:4–9)
>
> Remember this, keep it in mind,
> take it to heart, you rebels.
> Remember the former things, those of long ago;

I am God, and there is no other;
I am God, and there is none like me.
I make known the end from the beginning,
from ancient times, what is still to come.
I say, 'My purpose will stand,
and I will do all that I please.'
From the east I summon a bird of prey;
from a far-off land, a man to fulfill my purpose.
What I have said, that I will bring about;
what I have planned, that I will do.
Listen to me, you stubborn-hearted,
you who are now far from my righteousness.
I am bringing my righteousness near,
The word nigh thee (Romans 10:8–13)

A good man brings out the best in another person that has the same intention:

> No good tree bears bad fruit, nor does a bad tree bear good fruit. Each tree is recognized by its own fruit. People do not pick figs from thornbushes, or grapes from briers. A good man brings good things out of the good stored up in his heart, and an evil man brings evil things out of the evil stored up in his heart. For the mouth speaks what the heart is full of. (Luke 6:43–45)

# 24

## CHAPTER

*The fast that God accepted and the one he does not accept*

There are many scriptures that speak on the things that God does not accept while we're fasting and praying for God's help.

> Is it a fast that I have chosen,
> A day for a man to afflict his soul?
> Is it to bow down his head like a bulrush,
> And to spread out sackcloth and ashes?
> Would you call this a fast,
> And an acceptable day to the Lord?
> acceptable day to the Lord?
> Is this not the fast that I have chosen:
> To loose the bonds of wickedness, to undo the heavy burdens,
> To let the oppressed go free,
> And that you break every yoke?
> Is it not to share your bread with the hungry,
> And that you bring to your house the poor who are cast out;
> When you see the naked, that you cover him,
> And not hide yourself from your own flesh?
> Then your light shall break forth like the morning,
> Your healing shall spring forth speedily,
> And your righteousness shall go before you;

The glory of the Lord shall be your rear guard.
(Isaiah 58:8)

When they fast, I will not hear their cry; and
when they offer burnt offering and an oblation, I
will not accept them: but I will consume them by
the sword, and by the famine, and by the pesti-
lence. (Jeremiah 14:12)

Why have we fasted, say they, and you see
not? why have we afflicted our soul, and you take
no knowledge? Behold, in the day of your fast you
find pleasure, and exact all your labors.
Indeed you fast for strife and debate,
And to strike with the fist of wickedness.
You will not fast as you do this day,
To make your voice heard on high. (Isaiah
58:3)

# 25
# CHAPTER

*Two should not walk if they do not agree.*

My feet are on the ground now but almost slipped away before!

Surely God is good to Israel, to those who are pure in heart. But as for me, my feet had almost slipped; I had nearly lost my foothold. For I envied the arrogant when I saw the prosperity of the wicked. (Psalm 73:2)

Paul tells us to stand firm with our feet fitted with the readiness that comes from the gospel of peace. Having our shoes fitted with the gospel of peace allows us to do this successfully. (Ephesians 6:15)

Peace I leave with you; my peace I give you. I do not give to you as the world gives. (John 14:27)

# 26
## CHAPTER

*I am a wonder.*

f I started writing stories, people would be wondering how this person could be alive today. So I will only prick your curiosity on thinking about this, and what I would write about next!

As a little girl, growing up, I knew what I wanted, although I was just so very quiet. I would wake up and create a three-sixty-degree turn around on everyone! It may seem shocking to the person that reads this that at the tender age of seven, my uncle cooked something that I loved and said to me that I couldn't have any; he didn't know how much he made me feel sad inside.

I stood there, watching him with a sharp steer. There was not even a tear. I was not crying or smiling—just waiting. Alas! My uncle said, "Anyone wanted any of this food that I cooked?"

I said, "Me. And I am hungry!"

He said, "The only way you are getting any of this food today, you will have to eat it with all the wickedness that I am preparing in this food!"

I continued to look at him, so very naive as he filled the delicious plate of food with wickedness. I didn't know what wickedness was in those days!

I marveled today at this story because I have grown into grace when I think about the goodness of God!

Are you there? Are you still waiting and wondering what happened next? Stay tuned. I will be right back!

> Hear this word that the Lord hath spoken against you, O children of Israel, against the whole family which I brought up from the land of Egypt, saying,
>
> You only have I known of all the families of the earth: therefore I will punish you for all your iniquities.
>
> Can two walk together, except they be agreed?
>
> Will two people walk together unless they have agreed to do so?
>
> Will a lion roar in the forest, when he hath no prey? Will a young lion cry out of his den, if he have taken nothing?
>
> Can a bird fall in a snare upon the earth, where no gin is for him? shall one take up a snare from the earth, and have taken nothing at all?
> (Amos 3)

This was what I was waiting for when my uncle said, "I will put the plate down. And if you want it, you can eat it!"

I can only tell you that the thing that a child endured in the first years of growing up with a person that hasn't a clue about the goodness and love of God in their lives are strange but merciless to others! I know now that there's no other recourse to read just the pain of yesterday to today's joyful days where the Lord gives mercy to whomever he chooses!

Taking the plate of wickedness from where he put it was joyous for a child, thinking that they were getting a good deal out of the whole thing! But after consuming the lot of it, then came the turmoil of tears and screaming and rolling around on the ground because the plate of wickedness was hot peppers that couldn't be contained with just water after eating it! Are you still there?

I realized that I have overcome the obstacles even when I am very young!

I can tell you to go a mile in my shoes, but it will take a miracle for you to continue walking in them. I know that not everyone can fit in my shoes! Whenever I walk, I have seen things that will destroy the feet of people that take pride in their toes, and the pedicure that was done to give that everlasting glow of comfort would be destroy before one foot lift off the ground to take the first stride to follow in my footstep!

And the Lord spake unto Moses in the plains of Moab by Jordan near Jericho, saying,

Speak unto the children of Israel, and say unto them, When ye are passed over Jordan into the land of Canaan;

Then ye shall drive out all the inhabitants of the land from before you, and destroy all their pictures, and destroy all their molten images, and quite pluck down all their high places

And ye shall dispossess the inhabitants of the land, and dwell therein: for I have given you the land to possess it.

And ye shall divide the land by lot for an inheritance among your families: and to the more ye shall give the more inheritance, and to the fewer ye shall give the less inheritance: every man's inheritance shall be in the place where his lot falleth; according to the tribes of your fathers ye shall inherit.

But if ye will not drive out the inhabitants of the land from before you; then it shall come to pass, that those which ye let remain of them shall be pricks in your eyes, and thorns in your sides, and shall vex you in the land wherein ye dwell.

Moreover it shall come to pass, that I shall do unto you, as I thought to do unto them. (Numbers 33)

The Lord your God which goeth before you, he shall fight for you, according to all that he did for you in Egypt before your eyes;

And in the wilderness, where thou hast seen how that the Lord thy God bare thee, as a man doth bear his son, in all the way that ye went, until ye came into this place.

Yet in this thing ye did not believe the Lord your God,

Who went in the way before you, to search you out a place to pitch your tents in, in fire by night, to shew you by what way ye should go, and in a cloud by day.

And the Lord heard the voice of your words, and was wroth, and sware, saying,

Surely there shall not one of these men of this evil generation see that good land, which I sware to give unto your fathers.

Save Caleb the son of Jephunneh; he shall see it, and to him will I give the land that he hath trodden upon, and to his children, because he hath wholly followed the Lord.

Also the Lord was angry with me for your sakes, saying, Thou also shalt not go in thither.

But Joshua the son of Nun, which standeth before thee, he shall go in thither: encourage him: for he shall cause Israel to inherit it.

Moreover your little ones, which ye said should be a prey, and your children, which in that day had no knowledge between good and evil, they shall go in thither, and unto them will I give it, and they shall possess it.

But as for you, turn you, and take your journey into the wilderness by the way of the Red sea.

Then ye answered and said unto me, We have sinned against the Lord, we will go up and fight, according to all that the Lord our God commanded us. And when ye had girded on every man his weapons of war, ye were ready to go up into the hill. (Deuteronomy 1)

# 27
## CHAPTER

*Good and evil don't walk.*

The Bible says the steps of a good man are order by the Lord!

> The steps of a good man are ordered by the Lord: And he delighteth in his way. Though he fall, he shall not be utterly cast down: For the Lord upholdeth him with his hand. (Psalm 37:23–24 KJV)

Good is defined as the following:

> But the fruit of the Spirit is love, joy, peace, forbearance, kindness, goodness, faithfulness, gentleness and self-control. Against such things there is no law. (Galatians 5:22–23)

> Neither do people light a lamp and put it under a bowl. Instead they put it on its stand, and it gives light to everyone in the house. In the same way, let your light shine before others, that they may see your good deeds and glorify your Father in heaven. (Matthew 5:15–16)

"I have the right to do anything," you say—
but not everything is beneficial. "I have the right to
do anything"—but not everything is constructive.
(1 Corinthians 10:23)

# 28
## CHAPTER

When the wicked man/woman that you acquaint yourself with calls you, don't think for one minute that they call you to wish you well! Do you believe that they call to wish you long life? I know that they call me to see if their wickedness prevails over God anointing. Boy, they are so wrong!

This is like a system that nibbles you up in small pieces and spits you out as there's no digestive system that is there to allow you to be swallowed!

As the word of God said that it's not good for man to be alone, I left work with such good intentions—to take a few days off and enjoy the atmosphere in my life with my time in prayer with the Lord God Almighty because he is first, then my spouse!

I spoke to God and said, "This day, I have done so much for twenty years." I repeated myself to God and said, "The twenty years is too much, and I am done! If you want to keep him where he is, he belongs to you. He is yours, and it's all up to you! When he is ready to find me, he can find me in your arms!" I said I needed a turnaround today, not tomorrow with him, and went about my business!

I was in prayer when my phone rang. I didn't answer the call! After prayer, I heard my phone rang again, and I saw that it was Tom, and I answered it. He was frantic on the other side of the phone line. I was very calm. I was just listening. And he said to me, "Call Mary the home-wrecker." He used to have an affair with this person that is what he is telling me; could you imagine that she continues to pursue me even though she knew I was married!

I said, "What?"

He continued to explain to me that he deleted her number a while ago, but the bad sores kept coming back because she loved money. She had kept his number and kept calling him. He asked me to please call her. He explained, "She is afraid of you!" Men are so—

I leave the sentence for you to finish!

The wicked watcheth the righteous,
And seeketh to slay him.
The Lord will not leave him in his hand,
Nor condemn him when he is judged. (Psalm 37)

I said, "Now, God, what is this? I asked you to take care of one problem, and now I thought you fixed it." I was not applauding as I just finished a Zoom prayer. I picked up the phone, and I said, "In the mighty name of Jesus Christ of Nazareth, the true and living God, I break your power, Satan. I command the angels of the Lord God Almighty to draw the naked sword of the Lord and chapped up your altar. And may your food that you give your god become ashes before them!" I was not finished with her, but she hung up. So I dialed the number again and continued to pray that every Dagon godhead must be chopped off and rolled before the true and living God. Then I heard her curse something and said, "You, Jamaican." I started tongues of fire in the mighty name of Jesus. Then the line went dead!

"Not even five minutes later, Tom called me and said, "Thank you so much!" I really didn't care what he had experienced during this moment of my praying. All I knew was that she would never ever think about another extramarital affair again with anyone's husband! There would be some other man that would fall prey to this scavenger woman hunter, but she would not ever forget me and come back to me!

When all of these affairs started, no one had invited me to sit down and have lunch or dinner, not even a cup of tea. But now it was the time that they had me in mind when something went south, and things became sour. And then I was the main ingredients. They couldn't leave me out. They had to remember that they couldn't cook without the things that give the spice and sugar by the same person that was hurting me calling for my help! May God punish every devil and put fire in every home-wrecker's home and body today in the name of Jesus Christ, Son of the living God!

God agreed with me and answered my prayers. It has been months, and I can go about my business and not be worried because the snares has been broken and destroyed out of my marriage and life!

> I thank God, whom I serve with a pure con-
> science, as my forefathers did, as without ceasing I
> remember you in my prayers night and day, greatly
> desiring to see you, being mindful of your tears, that
> I may be filled with joy, when I call to remembrance
> the genuine faith that is in you, which dwelt first
> in your grandmother Lois and your mother Eunice,
> and I am persuaded is in you also. Therefore I
> remind you to stir up the gift of God which is in
> you through the laying on of my hands. For God
> has not given us a spirit of fear, but of power and of
> love and of a sound mind. (2 Timothy 1:3)

> And why do you worry about clothes? See
> how the flowers of the field grow. They do not
> labor or spin. Yet I tell you that not even Solomon
> in all his splendor was dressed like one of these.
> If that is how God clothes the grass of the field,
> which is here today and tomorrow is thrown into
> the fire, will he not much more clothe you—you
> of little faith? So do not worry, saying, 'What shall
> we eat?' or 'What shall we drink?' or 'What shall
> we wear?' For the pagans run after all these things,
> and your heavenly Father knows that you need
> them. But seek first his kingdom and his righ-
> teousness, and all these things will be given to you
> as well. Therefore do not worry about tomorrow,
> for tomorrow will worry about itself. Each day has
> enough trouble of its own. (Matthews 6)

# 29
## CHAPTER

said, "Daddy, Papa Jesus, every time you give me a revelation, I am in the restroom! You know we are off to stop meeting like this." I can't control my laughter!

If you make your bed in hell, behold, I am there!

> Where can I go from Your Spirit? Or where can I flee from Your presence? If I ascend into heaven, You are there; If I make my bed in hell, behold, You are there. If I take the wings of the morning, And dwell in the uttermost parts of the sea, Even there Your hand shall lead me, And Your right hand shall hold me.
>
> While there is no verse that says "a third of the angels fell from heaven," some verses, when put together, lead us to that conclusion. Sometime after their creation. (Psalm 139:7–12 NKJV)
>
> His tail swept down a third of the stars of heaven and cast them to the earth. And the dragon stood before the woman who was about to give birth, so that when she bore her child he might devour it. (Revelation 12:4)

And he said to them, "I saw Satan fall like lightning from heaven." (Luke 10:18)

And the great dragon was thrown down, that ancient serpent, who is called the devil and Satan, the deceiver of the whole world—he was thrown down to the earth, and his angels were thrown down with him. (Revelation 12:9)

For if God did not spare angels when they sinned, but cast them into hell and committed them to chains of gloomy darkness to be kept until the judgment. (2 Peter 2:4)

See, I have set before thee this day life and good, and death and evil;

In that I command thee this day to love the Lord thy God, to walk in his ways, and to keep his commandments and his statutes and his judgments, that thou mayest live and multiply: and the Lord thy God shall bless thee in the land whither thou goest to possess it.

But if thine heart turn away, so that thou wilt not hear, but shalt be drawn away, and worship other gods, and serve them;

I denounce unto you this day, that ye shall surely perish, and that ye shall not prolong your days upon the land, whither thou passest over Jordan to go to possess it.

I call heaven and earth to record this day against you, that I have set before you life and death, blessing and cursing: therefore choose life, that both thou and thy seed may live:

That thou mayest love the Lord thy God, and that thou mayest obey his voice, and that thou mayest cleave unto him: for he is thy life, and the length of thy days: that thou mayest dwell in the land which the Lord sware unto thy fathers, to Abraham, to Isaac, and to Jacob, to give them. (Deuteronomy 30:15–20)

# 30
## CHAPTER

*Prayers answer and the prayers that are not answered*

*Unanswered prayer*

> You ask and do not receive, because you ask with wrong motives, so that you may spend it on your pleasures. (James 4:3)

> If I regard wickedness in my heart,
> The Lord will not hear. (Psalm 66:18)

> But your iniquities have made a separation between you and your God,
> And your sins have hidden His face from you so that He does not hear. (Isaiah 59:2, source: https://bible.knowing-jesus.com/topics/Unanswered-Prayer)

> Thou hast also given me the necks of mine enemies; that I might destroy them that hate me.
> They cried, but there was none to save them: even unto the Lord, but he answered them not.
> Then did I beat them small as the dust before the wind: I did cast them out as the dirt in the streets. (Psalm 18:40–42)

was having a conversation today with a friend of mine. It was very interesting to speak to someone who has the same faith in God as I have! I was asking her about some invitation that I have, but I would like to extend it to other people who would like to come under my invitation.

I asked her if she knew anyone else who would like to come to the Three Days of Glory and the encounter for the weekend of August 13 through 16, 2021. The answer was so shocking but true! She said, "My dear sister, you know that people don't love the Lord like that to give up their weekend and go to those places! You know that those things are not appealing to them." I marveled at the idea of a person who takes God for granted; and only when they are in trouble, they remember that God exists!

> If you remain in Me and My Words remain in you, ask whatever you wish, and it will be done for you. (John 15:7)

> Therefore I tell you, whatever you ask for in prayer, believe that you have received it, and it will be yours. (Mark 11:24)

> Do not be anxious about anything, but in every situation, by prayer and petition, with thanksgiving, present your requests to God. (Philippians 4:6)

> We know that God does not listen to sinners. He listens to the godly person who does his will. (John 9:31)

> For the eyes of the Lord are on the righteous and his ears are attentive to their prayer, but the face of the Lord is against those who do evil. (1 Peter 3:12)

> And if we know that he hears us—whatever
> we ask—we know that we have what we asked of
> him. (1 John 5:15)

> Then you will call on me and come and pray
> to me, and I will listen to you. You will seek me
> and find me when you seek me with all your heart.
> (Jeremiah 29:12–13)

Jesus said to ask, and it will be given us (Matthew 7:7). In order for our prayers to be answered though, we must heed the advice our good Lord gave us in His Word. He told Solomon, "If My people, who are called by My Name, will humble themselves and pray and seek My face, and turn from their wicked ways, then I will hear from Heaven and I will forgive their sin and heal their land" (2 Chronicles 7:14). Similarly, Jesus said in John 15:7 that if we abide in Him, then He will abide in us. Yes, there are conditions to having our prayers answered.

> Confess your faults one to another, and pray
> one for another, that ye may be healed. The effec-
> tual fervent prayer of a righteous man availeth
> much. (James 5:16)

> But when you ask, you must believe and not
> doubt, because the one who doubts is like a wave
> of the sea, blown and tossed by the wind. (James
> 1:6)

> Another angel, who had a golden censer,
> came and stood at the altar. He was given much
> incense to offer, with the prayers of all God's peo-
> ple, on the golden altar in front of the throne. The
> smoke of the incense, together with the prayers of
> God's people, went up before God from the angel's
> hand. Then the angel took the censer, filled it with

fire from the altar, and hurled it on the earth; and there came peals of thunder, rumblings, flashes of lightning and an earthquake. (Revelation 8:3–5)

# 31
# CHAPTER

*The gifts that God gave*

**N**ow, concerning spiritual gifts, brethren, I do not want you to be unaware.

> But to each one is given the manifestation of the Spirit for the common good. (1 Corinthians 12:7)

> Pursue love, yet desire earnestly spiritual gifts, but especially that you may prophesy. (1 Corinthians 14:1)

> Now there are varieties of gifts, but the same Spirit. (1 Corinthians 12:4)

> Since we have gifts that differ according to the grace given to us, each of us is to exercise them accordingly: if prophecy, according to the proportion of his faith;
> have filled him with the Spirit of God in wisdom, in understanding, in knowledge, and in all kinds of craftsmanship. (Romans 12:6, source: https://bible.knowing-jesus.com/topics/Spiritual-Gifts)

So that you are not lacking in any gift, awaiting eagerly the revelation of our Lord Jesus Christ. (1 Corinthians 1:7)

If I have the gift of prophecy, and know all mysteries and all knowledge; and if I have all faith, so as to remove mountains, but do not have love, I am nothing. (1 Corinthians 13:2)

Now when Simon saw that the Spirit was bestowed through the laying on of the apostles' hands, he offered them money. (Acts 8:18)

But to each one of us grace was given according to the measure of Christ's gift. (Ephesians 4:7)

For this reason I remind you to kindle afresh the gift of God which is in you through the laying on of my hands. (2 Timothy 1:6)

Now we have received, not the spirit of the world, but the Spirit who is from God, so that we may know the things freely given to us by God. (1 Corinthians 2:12)

So then tongues are for a sign, not to those who believe but to unbelievers; but prophecy is for a sign, not to unbelievers but to those who believe. (1 Corinthians 14:22)

The Spirit of the Lord will rest on Him,
The spirit of wisdom and understanding,
The spirit of counsel and strength,
The spirit of knowledge and the fear of the Lord. (Isaiah 11:2)

for the gifts and the calling of God are irrevocable. (Romans 11:29)

If service, in his serving; or he who teaches, in his teaching. (Romans 12:7)

If we sowed spiritual things in you, is it too much if we reap material things from you? (1 Corinthians 9:11)

That in everything you were enriched in Him, in all speech and all knowledge. (1 Corinthians 1:5)

Therefore I make known to you that no one speaking by the Spirit of God says, "Jesus is accursed"; and no one can say, "Jesus is Lord," except by the Holy Spirit. (1 Corinthians 12:3)

This is the only thing I want to find out from you: did you receive the Spirit by the works of the Law, or by hearing with faith? (Galatians 3:2)

Now you are Christ's body, and individually members of it. (1 Corinthians 12:27)

Which things we also speak, not in words taught by human wisdom, but in those taught by the Spirit, combining spiritual thoughts with spiritual words. (1 Corinthians 2:13)

God also testifying with them, both by signs and wonders and by various miracles and by gifts of the Holy Spirit according to His own will. (Hebrews 2:4)

But a natural man does not accept the things of the Spirit of God, for they are foolishness to him; and he cannot understand them, because they are spiritually appreciated. (1 Corinthians 2:14)

Paul said, "John baptized with the baptism of repentance, telling the people to believe in Him who was coming after him, that is, in Jesus." When they heard this, they were baptized in the name of the Lord Jesus. And when Paul had laid his hands upon them, the Holy Spirit came on them, and they began speaking with tongues and prophesying. (Acts 19:4–6)

For just as we have many members in one body and all the members do not have the same function, so we, who are many, are one body in Christ, and individually members one of another. Since we have gifts that differ according to the grace given to us, each of us is to exercise them accordingly: if prophecy, according to the proportion of his faith; read more. (Romans 12:4–8)

Now concerning spiritual gifts, brethren, I do not want you to be unaware. You know that when you were pagans, you were led astray to the mute idols, however you were led. Therefore I make known to you that no one speaking by the Spirit of God says, "Jesus is accursed"; and no one can say, "Jesus is Lord," except by the Holy Spirit. read more. (1 Corinthians 12:1–11)

*Topics on spiritual gifts—diversity of spiritual gifts*

> Now there are varieties of gifts, but the same Spirit. (1 Corinthians 12:4–6)

*Spiritual gifts given to church*

> And He gave some as apostles, and some as prophets, and some as evangelists, and some as pastors and teachers. (Ephesians 4:11)

*Spiritual gifts, importance of love*

> If I speak with the tongues of men and of angels, but do not have love, I have become a noisy gong or a clanging cymbal. (1 Corinthians 13:1)

> Therefore, my brethren, desire earnestly to prophesy, and do not forbid to speak in tongues. (1 Corinthians 14:39, Source: https://bible.knowing-jesus.com/topics/Spiritual-Gifts)

# 32
## CHAPTER

*Man to man*

Man is so unjust to one another that when the goodness of God is working in one's life, it is not God. They say this has to be a devil they're using! I have seen the work of miracle of God work in people's lives. And at the time of the manifestation, the joy cannot be contained. When the devil shows up, it takes only one devil to start a domino effect, and the same person that receives that miracle from God begins to waver their faith! There is no good thing that comes from the devil. It may seem that something good just happens when a person with bad intention hands you something that appears to be good. Then the true intention behind it appears, and all things become a problem because it is not good in the first place. But your eyes just open to see that it is covered with a vale or shell.

> But every man is tempted, when he is drawn away of his own lust, and enticed.
> Then when lust hath conceived, it bringeth forth sin: and sin, when it is finished, bringeth forth death.
> Do not err, my beloved brethren.
> Every good gift and every perfect gift is from above, and cometh down from the Father of lights, with whom is no variableness, neither shadow of turning. (James 1)

If any of you lack wisdom, let him ask of God, that giveth to all men liberally, and upbraideth not; and it shall be given him. (James 1)

All good things and perfect things come from above!
Faith is an anchor that when it is launched, you cannot pull back!
If your faith is dead, you will need mine!
Now is the time to separate the sheep from the goats.

Henceforth there is laid up for me the crown of righteousness, which the Lord, the righteous judge, will award to me on that Day, and not only to me but also to all who have loved his appearing. (2 Timothy 4:8)

And these will go away into eternal punishment, but the righteous into eternal life. (Matthew 25:46)

Behold, all souls are mine; the soul of the father as well as the soul of the son is mine: the soul who sins shall die. (Ezekiel 18:4)

Take the water of life without price.

Then I saw a new heaven and a new earth, for the first heaven and the first earth had passed away, and the sea was no more. And I saw the holy city, new Jerusalem, coming down out of heaven from God, prepared as a bride adorned for her husband. And I heard a loud voice from the throne saying, "Behold, the dwelling place of God is with man. He will dwell with them, and they will be his people, and God himself will be with them as their God. He will wipe away every tear from their eyes, and death shall be no more, neither shall there be mourning, nor crying, nor pain anymore, for the former things have passed away." And he who was seated on the throne said, "Behold, I am making all things new." Also he said, Write this down, for these words are trustworthy and true." (Revelation 21:1–27)

From Matthew 25:31–46: "But when the Son of Man comes in his glory, and all the holy angels with him, then he will sit on the throne of his glory. Before him all the nations will be gathered, and he will separate them one from another, as a shepherd separates the sheep from the goats."

*Change your lifestyle and do not stay in with their company.*

# 33
## CHAPTER

*I have learned!*

There are a lot of things that people used to get to where they are going because it is the only way they know how! I have been in the street and walking in lane that leads to places that don't have good streets or directions to the place where we're going when you are trusting in God.

If you have not been in these streets and walked in those lanes, you will not be able to fit in the same shoes that I have put on and walk in! The chapters written in the book are totally different!

The only reason why we are aware of this is because halfway there, we encountered thing that was not in the equation. The good news is that I'm not worried about the things in life that God has in his hands as I know that he has already cleared the way! I will go before you and make every crooked way straight. I know who is watching my back, so I can't remember thinking about my back because it's covered!

Jamaica is saying, "Back a dog is dog! Before dog is Mr. Dog!"

# 34
## CHAPTER

*I have walked*

There was so much problem in my life spiritually, I didn't know whether I was going or coming; so I decided that I would seek help from places that do prayers! I went to a priest. And as he saw me, he told me that he could not help me because people who he had seen with my problems are dead!

I have been to places before that make you still believe that you are totally in Christ. I have learned that when you go to an altar, it is a place of exchange! When I realized that the problem that was affecting me in my life was not just physical, I went to church. And when I would leave that church, I would sometimes ask the Lord to take off the things I felt on my head. I would be watching my head with holy water, then I was fine. But whenever I came home, I would be fighting devils that had nothing to do with the plan of God in my life!

People who were there in my life to create a harmonious relationship with me, and God had failed me yet again as they had done so to others before, I visited the priest, and the stench of evil was so pronounced that, as he looked at me, he said, "I can't help you!"

I said, "God brought me."

He said, "Oh, Lord, if the Lord sent you, I'll put myself and family at risk."

He then turned to me and said that Jesus saved me in the hospital when I was much younger. After praying with him, I got some relief and left! I brought him a Bible after I got the relief that I was looking for. And when he was going away, he said that he had reached the airport and forgotten the Bible and said that he remembered and turned back for his Bible that I gave him, saying all of this to bring you to this level as there are levels and levels! I was not aware that he had gone to Canada for emergency trips, and I went to look for him, and there was another priest there.

I was speaking to him, and he told me that he saw so much light around me, and I didn't say anything to him as he continued to speak to me and ask me to pray for him. I wish I had the revelations that God gave me to know that then. I can tell you what you don't know: It can make you or break your willpower! I didn't understand it or get it until I was in the city, and the priest that I went to the first time called me from a different telephone number and asked me to pray with him because he was fighting with some devil that was difficult for him, and then I did pray with him!

I was getting too comfortable with these people. I realized that the manipulation of a sweet talk can either draw you closer the devil or put extra distance between you and those who think that you are not aware of the plots of the devil's plans. When I got there one day and they let me know that whenever I come to their home, I brought so much light. This was it. Just as I sat down, I was talking with this other priest, and he said to me, "I was praying for you last night, and I saw you with wings!"

I realized that all this time, I was endowed with a supernatural blessing from God. But I was not tapping into the right frequency that could catapult me to my next level in God!

I was too laid back and depended on people who have their own agendas. You give me something, but I'm going to take double times what you are getting. The only thing is that you can't see what you are exchanging for your return to their altars.

Altars are a place of exchange!

The Bible asks if there's anything you want to exchange for your soul after gaining the world! The only reason that I didn't give up much was because I didn't want anything. Even the priest said to me one day, "You are the only person who comes here and does not want to accept anything!"

I said, "I don't need anything!"

> For what shall it profit a man, if he shall gain the whole world, and lose his own soul? (Mark 8:34–38)

I looked at him and smiled, knowing that this was my last day coming to sit down with him as I had been waiting for the different levels of elevation, and I was higher than him! I have never returned back to them because the priest that I was sent to is no longer there! There are levels and levels!

# 35
## CHAPTER

*Trouble and trouble*

O ne of my brothers always called me. And whenever he called me, it would be, "Sis, I am in trouble!"

"What is going on with you?" I said.

He said, "Please pray for me. I got a car to rent, and the car crashed. And the owner wanted me to pay them three hundred thousand dollars."

I said, "What? Didn't they have insurance on the car!"

He said, "Yes."

I told him to take heart, and I was going to pray! The next time my brother called me, a month after, he said, "Sis, I am going to court, and I will call you later."

I said to him, "Call me when you are there!"

My brother was in court and called me, and I prayed. Ten minutes later, he called me and said, "Sis, they dismissed the case!"

I said, "I know!"

This is an ongoing thing. This is a continuing process with my brother. This time, he called me and said, "Sis, I need fifteen thousand to pay for a damage I caused by hitting someone's car, and they're asking me to pay them that amount!"

I said, "Okay, I'll send you the money. And when you get this money, the rest is to go to the altar of God!"

He said, "Yes, sis!"

Two months later, I got a call, and it was one of the biggest troubles he had ever encountered. And I said to him, "After this trouble that you get yourself into, please stay away from trouble!"

He was crying, and I felt what he was feeling. So I did what God does best, and I prayed that this too shall pass. And the final day of this situation in court again, he walked out in triumphed as God gave us the victory again!

Have you ever heard of "The last straw is the straw that broke the camel's back"? Well I was feeling like the camels now. My brother called me and said, "Sis, I am in trouble."

And before he could finish saying what he wanted to say, I said to him, "Don't you see that the place where you are is not good enough for you?"

There's never a dull moment with him!

"There's always something going on there, but you are the source of the energy that it's using! I am going on to remind you that Satan was falling from heaven like lightning. He's like a roaring lion, and this is not the plan of God for you! Now you listen to me carefully, trouble likes troubles. And when you attach yourself to trouble, it likes trouble. So do me a favor and stay away from trouble!"

> Yet man is born unto trouble, as the sparks fly upward. (Job 5:7)

> Man that is born of a woman is of few days and full of trouble.
>
> He cometh forth like a flower, and is cut down: he fleeth also as a shadow, and continueth not.
>
> And doth thou open thine eyes upon such an one, and bringest me into judgment with thee?
>
> Who can bring a clean thing out of an unclean? not one.
>
> Seeing his days are determined, the number of his months are with thee, thou hast appointed his bounds that he cannot pass;

Turn from him, that he may rest, till he shall
accomplish, as an hireling, his day. (Job 14)

Everyone's asking me, "Why don't you take the COVID-19 vaccination?"

I said to them, "I know. Everyone wants to be first, but I don't mind in this case. I don't mind waiting. I can be last!"

Delay is not denial as I am aware of the process of these things. I have come a long way to reach this point in my life!

# 36
## CHAPTER

*Walk of insecurity*

I arose to the bright light of the sun shining through the window shade as I turned over in my bed and looked at the clock to see that the time has gone when I should be out of bed already. *Oh my, it's that time,* I thought, *because I had just closed my eyes for an hour only before I looked at the clock.* I got out of bed for another devotion, seeking God's face before I faced the world and got my affairs in order for the journey ahead of me as I went to my home!

*Pros and cons of insecurity*

Do you feel insecure? Many people feel insecure at some point, but most of them do not know it. It is normal to feel insecure. Most individuals can resolve feelings of insecurity before they have a harmful impact. However, if it occurs repeatedly over time, it can have dire consequences on your life. Feelings of insecurity come about when we have self-doubt, we feel anxious, we lack confidence, or we are uncertain about ourselves or our future. Insecurity has to do with the feelings we get or have that make us believe that we are not good enough. It relates to our feeling of uncertainty and inadequacy, which generates anxiety about our ability to cope with specific situations, relationships, and realizing our life goals. Buck (2012) carried out a research where he found that every individual at some point deals with insecurity, which manifests itself in all realms of life—social conditioning involving an individual observing others, their previous experiences, and traumatic events.

I believe this to be true because at some point I have had to deal with insecurities that originated from my local environments including home, work, and school. I have come across some people in my line of duty, individuals whose insecurities originate from general instability, and they experience unpredictable upsets throughout their lives. It is without a doubt that those individuals who experience recurring levels of insecurity tend to lack direction in life, have low self-esteem, experience body image issues, or feel overlooked by others. Buck (2012) said that coping with uncertainties requires us to identify the types of insecurity and their causes. It is also necessary for us to remind ourselves frequently about positive attributes and goals whenever we experience negative thoughts. Furthermore, in order to cope with psychological insecurities, reflect on your achievements and successes and eliminate a perfectionist attitude by practicing self-acceptance.

Do not be anxious about anything, but in every situation, by prayer and petition, with thanksgiving, present your requests to God. And the peace of God, which transcends all understanding, will guard your hearts and your minds in Christ Jesus. (Philippians 4:6–7)

Therefore do not be anxious, saying, "What shall we eat?" or "What shall we drink?" or "What shall we wear?" For the Gentiles seek after all these things, and your heavenly Father knows that you need them all. But seek first the kingdom of God and his righteousness, and all these things will be added to you. Therefore do not be anxious about tomorrow, for tomorrow will be anxious for itself. Sufficient for the day is its own trouble. (Matthew 6:31–34)

*Pros*

Despite the idea that insecurity negatively affects our mental health by feeding mental illnesses such as anxiety, low self-esteem, and depression, it has several advantages, including self-improvement. The primary advantage of insecurity that I have experienced in as far as my personality goes is that it sparks growth. Insecurity and self-improvement are directly correlated in that it pushes and jolts people toward achieving higher objectives. I have come across studies, which show that insecurity is advantageous when people begin to compare their weakest link to another person's strongest links. In such a scenario, an individual's assessment of their confidence triggers them to exclude the totality of who they are, thereby concentrating narrowly on the aspects of themselves that motivate them toward growth. This is true because at some point, when I was just starting my career, I would assess my insecurities inaccurately, and this lowered my level of confidence, thereby depriving myself of the ability to realize my goals or move forward. Instead of the insecurities functioning as a catalyst, they became fundamental in paralyzing my growth.

However, with time, I learned that if I accurately assessed the uncertainties I was having, I would be able to view someone else's achievements accurately, and this made me realize that greater goals are possible for me as well. Therefore, realistic self-doubt or insecurity is beneficial as it serves as a motivating force in pushing a person toward the urge to want to improve.

Vanderkam (2013) stated that when someone is dissatisfied with themselves and have a self-awareness of their limitations, they become open to feedback about improving themselves. In my case, I became aware of the things I needed to practice toward my growth. The more anxious or insecure I was regarding my upsides, the more I moved toward making smarter life decisions. As such, insecurity helped me to have self-awareness as it enhanced my confidence and pushed me to accomplish my goals.

An insecure personality improves one's safety. When I am uncertain about what I am likely to encounter, I become more cautious about events in my surroundings. This not only improves my safety but also my chance of survival as I scan my environment for any signs of danger. As Abbate-Daga et al. (2010) stated, insecurity or a person's anticipation for a precarious future significantly contributes to caution, thus making the individual aspire to avoid injuries and accidents. For example, it would be riskier for me to walk in an open field during a thunderstorm, holding a metal golf club overhead even when the chances of being struck by lightning are minimal. As such, insecure people have a higher likelihood to survive swindle motives. Rarely do insecure individuals trust other individuals, and this reluctance has made many of us doubt the intentions of those who want to take advantage of us. For instance, I have been able to avoid signing an unfair contract.

Nonetheless, with self-awareness, I have been able to balance my level of uncertainty to moderate where I conduct a detailed assessment of the contracts to determine whether the contract is genuine. Therefore, while an insecure personality improved my safety by helping me scan my surroundings for potential dangers, it also helped me to avoid deceptive actions by others.

I have also observed that overconfidence makes some people immune to negative feedback. This implies that less confident individuals are more likely to accept criticism as constructive. Additionally, insecure individuals strive to improve their weaknesses and hence boost their self-esteem and self-confidence in pursuing life goals.

A reasonable level of insecurity about people or events leads to reflection and self-improvement. If you desire to better your personality or relationships with others, your ability to moderate high level of insecurity and achieve a balance with self-awareness is fundamental in motivating you to improve not only yourself but also your relationships with others. Thus, I have realized that there is a need for me to have a balance between confidence and insecurity for me to be successful in life.

Insecurity is directly linked to self-awareness. People who have a relatively high level of self-awareness are usually less insecure as they understand their personality, emotions, and emotional attachment with others. Self-awareness is crucial as it reduces insecurity, as it makes us not to compare ourselves with others.

Many of us face the challenge of measuring ourselves against certain arbitrary standards that other members of society set. This affects healthy living and our relationship with others.

Insecure people tend to be humble and empathetic. From my experience, insecurity encourages individuals to be grateful, to appreciate the value of the gift of love, and to be humble. Realizing empathy in life can be difficult unless a person recognizes personal vulnerabilities and identify others who are less fortunate. Even though confidence defines people as being charismatic or charming, over-confidence makes others label them as being arrogant, particularly when the confidence is considered to be unwarranted. Therefore, in efforts to avoid overconfidence, many people practice the culture of being insecure while interacting with others. Thus, the virtue of being insecure makes most of us appear modest and humble in such interactions, thereby improving our self-esteem.

I have also found that childhood experiences are crucial in determining an adult's level of insecurity. Children's experiences are fundamental to their emotional development. As parents, we act as primary attachment figures and determines how our children experience the world as we help them understand the ups and downs of how their lives would be like. Insecurity helps the children recognize these challenges and determine whether the world would be a safe place for them to explore or take emotional risks. This is so given that insecure people have a higher likelihood to ascertain whether they will be hurt or meet untrustworthy people. Stinson (2010) argued that the virtue of being insecure ensures that individuals learn about the most significant people in their lives who would be crucial in supporting them when they encounter emotional needs.

And in Christ, you have been brought to fullness. He is the head over every power and authority. (Colossians 2:10)

Have I not commanded you? Be strong and courageous. Do not be afraid; do not be discouraged, for the Lord your God will be with you wherever you. (Joshua 1:9)

Therefore, since we have been justified through faith, we have peace with God through our Lord Jesus Christ, through whom we have gained access by faith into this grace in which we now stand. And we boast in the hope of the glory of God. (Romans 5:1–2)

Insecurity is also directly related to trauma. Research shows that children who grew up in emotionally, physically, and sexually abusive environments seem to be insecure. The absence of the secure attachment realm while growing up makes individuals grow up into adults who struggle with emotions of low self-esteem, low self-worth, and difficulty in realizing self-worth. It is however important to understand that despite insecurity laying a foundation of increased risk of insecure people to develop anxiety and depression, such people are more likely to survive traumatic events, experiences, and environments.

# 37
## CHAPTER

*The cons*

It may be difficult for an individual with high insecurity levels to form long-lasting relations or take part in daily activities due to a self-perception of inadequacy and helplessness (Barling and Kelloway 2016). When I was facing insecurities years back, I would get all feelings, and they made me have negative thoughts regarding my ability to fit in with friends, peers, reach my goal in life, and find support as well as acceptance. With insecurity comes anxiety. I would experience feelings of fear, uneasiness, and self-doubt, all of which characterize anxiety, which made me feel that I was not well equipped to deal with the challenges of life, therefore, I felt helpless. Apart from struggling to form healthy relations, I found it hard to share my emotions or be straightforward with important daily-life aspects like those relating to school or work. People who cannot speak about their accomplishments and abilities because they are too anxious or feel insecure may never be promoted at work, which may further promote insecurity attributable to a perceived lack of ability, which was true in my case.

I have come across people with chronic insecurity, and they are often too shy to face people. They not only find it difficult to form relationships but also meet others, which results in estrangement from people. Such distancing, as Buck et al. (2012) explained, results in isolation, an aspect that is related to mental health conditions like borderline personality, poor body image, paranoia, dependent personalities, low self-esteem, and narcissism. Let me use an example of a borderline personality because I have come across many people in the line of work diagnosed with BPD. The most troublesome and deepest part of borderline personality disorder (BPD) is insecurity evident through nagging and unsettling behavior. The insecurity that people with BPD feel dictates not only their actions but also beliefs, behaviors, thoughts, and their association with others. Therefore, part of the insecurity that such individuals feel transforms into obsessive egoistical self-hatred demonstrated through eccentric behavior, clinginess in relationships, preoccupation with all that is wrong with oneself, such that the uncertainty and self-loathing generate dramatic episodes.

Additionally, for BPD, insecurity transforms to suspicion, paranoia, impulsivity, and verbal abuse. Such individuals often feel like everyone is plotting against them, bad-mouthing them, setting a trap for them, scheming to punish or expose them, thus, they find it hard to trust anybody. The closer a person is to them, the harder it is to maintain the relationship because when such an individual has been betrayed, insulted, or lied to, their suspicion and paranoia shoot up. Combined with the self-contempt and insecurities experienced, such individuals can lash out at others or themselves (Livesley 2011). Given that they find it difficult to generate emotions, thus lack self-control, BPDs act on emotional impulsivity. They get suicidal thoughts; engage in substance abuse, self-harm, or any spontaneous thrill-seeking behaviors such as compulsive shopping, tattoos, promiscuous sex, and piercings. Hence, in as much as such impulsive behaviors allow them to express a high amount of emotions and energy, it feeds their constant cycle of insecurity, which further contributes to lack of identity and self-hatred.

Likewise, individuals with social insecurity feel insecure when it comes to their association with others. There are so many ways that insecurities cause problems in people's relationships as I have explained earlier. According to Becke, a wellness and health expert at Maple Holistics, "being somewhat insecure or a little jealous/paranoid is natural. We can be very possessive, sometimes without even meaning it. You can think of all kinds of things, and it does not necessarily guide your decisions. However, this changes when you start acting on your insecurities. If you don't keep your insecurities in check, you may become too dependent on your partner" (Howard 2018). Due to insecurity, an individual may find it difficult to trust their partner, and this causes major problems given that mutual trust is an essential aspect of a healthy relationship. It is difficult for a person to open up to their partner emotionally if they do not trust them, and this may stunt the relationship's growth. Insecurities can also make an individual internalize the negative thoughts and act on them. It is not wrong to have negative thoughts, but I learned that if they happen frequently, and you put yourself down and internalize them, you can change the way you treat/act around your partner, and this is bound to affect the relationship. For instance, if an individual keeps saying things that make them feel pathetic, weak, and helpless, they begin to feel like it, which eventually affects your partner.

Insecurity can make you yearn for reassurance from your partner regularly. This is not a bad thing. However, if you keep longing for constant reassurance, the partner may get tired of reassuring you, which may cause more insecurity. Moreover, the fact that your partner grows tired of being there for you means that you are leaning on them heavily and not doing much for themselves. According to Clarke, "You don't feel adequate enough, and you look to your partner to redefine this for you when, all along, you are looking for something that comes from within radical self-acceptance." This may end up creating a feeling of distance in the relationship, which is dangerous as the essence of being in a relationship is to feel an emotional closeness with your spouse. You may even begin reading into the words of your partner in a manner that reinforces the insecurities you already have.

Insecurity also increases failure and rejection. When you encounter traumatic or discouraging phenomena and experiences in your lives, your mood becomes affected, particularly how you feel about yourself. Psychological studies on happiness suggest that approximately 40 percent of people's "happiness quotient" is linked to their recent failures (Howard, 2018). Most individuals have felt rejected by their family members or the society based on their past. This not only affects their self-esteem but also their relationships with others. For instance, following the death of their spouse, job loss, and negative health events, some people become insecure and unhappy, which ultimately leads to self-rejection, lower self-esteem, and a diminished sense of emotional well-being (Howard, 2018). As such, rejection based on insecurity leads most individuals to perceive themselves and others negatively, which eventually culminates in them being more reactive to failure.

Uncertainty also compels you to lack confidence because of social anxiety. Many of us usually lack confidence in social scenarios, such as dates, interviews, family gatherings, and parties. The lack of confidence, which is perpetrated through the fear of others evaluating their personality and character, causes us to feel self-conscious and anxious. Anxiety based on insecurity causes one to avoid social interactions, especially when they are anticipating social events or feeling uncomfortable while interacting with others. Experiences can also affect your sense of belonging whereby you don't feel as though you are good enough, interesting, or important. Although this type of insecurity is entirely founded on the individual's self-consciousness, it eventually affects their self-worth, thereby affecting their sense of belonging during social interactions. Insecure people also tend to exhibit eating disorders, like bulimia and anorexia, in addition to body image issues. In this case, eating disorders originate from a person being insecure about certain life situations or their appearance.

There is no fear in love, but perfect love casts out fear. For fear has to do with punishment, and whoever fears has not been perfected in love. (1 John 4:18)

Peace I leave with you; my peace I give to you. Not as the world gives do I give to you. Let not your hearts be troubled, neither let them be afraid. (John 14:27)

For we are God's handiwork, created in Christ Jesus to do good works, which God prepared in advance for us to do. (Ephesians 2:10)

## References

Abbate-Daga, G., Gramaglia, C., Federico, A., Marzola, E., and Secondo, F. (2010). "Attachment Insecurity, Personality, and Body Dissatisfaction in Eating Disorders." The Journal of Nervous and Mental Disease, 198(7), 520–524. doi: 10.1097/NMD.0b013e3181e4c6f7.

Barling, J., and Kelloway, E. K. (2016). "Job Insecurity and Health: The Moderating Role of Workplace Control." Stress and Health, 12(4), 253–259. Retrieved from https://onlinelibrary.wiley.com/doi/abs/10.1002/(SICI)1099-1700(199610)12:4%3C253::AID-SMI710%3E3.0.CO;2-2.

Buck, N. M., Leenaars, E. P., Emmelkamp P. M., and van Marle, H. J. (April 30, 2012). Explaining the Relationship between Insecure Attachment and Partner Abuse: The Role of Personality Characteristics." Journal of Interpersonal Violence, 27(16), 3149–3170. doi: 10.1177/0886260512441258.

Howard, L. (2018). "7 Signs Your Insecurities Are Causing Problems In Your Relationship." Retrieved from https://www.bustle.com/p/7-signs-your-insecurities-are-affecting-your-relationship-according-to-experts-9119211.

Livesley, W. J., Schroeder, M. L., and Jackson, D. N. (2010). "Dependent Personality Disorder and Attachment Problems." Journal of Personality Disorders, 4(2), 131–140. Retrieved from https://guilfordjournals.com/doi/abs/10.1521/pedi.1990.4.2.131.

Stinson, D. A. (August 15, 2011). Psychologists Interrupt the Miserable Cycle of Social Insecurity." Association for Psychological Science. Retrieved from https://www.psychologicalscience.org/news/releases/psychologists-interrupt-the-miserable-cycle-of-social-insecurity.html.

Vanderkam., L. (November 25, 2013). "Why Insecurity May Be the Key To Success." Fast Company. Retrieved from https://www.fastcompany.com/3022152/why-insecurity-may-be-the-key-to-success.

# 38
## CHAPTER

*Unmerited favor and obedience walk together.*

I encountered a problem when the mortgage company sent me a letter to let me know that my second mortgage matured! "Mature," I said to myself as I did not consider that the second mortgage could be such a pain. Fifteen years younger than the primary mortgage, so they reminded me! I tried to get help from within the company that had my primary mortgage to refinance the second mortgage as they took information to do the refinance. I waited for months and was still hoping to get it done fast. Then on the first of December 2020, they sent me a letter to let me know that they could not help me. I called different companies as my husband is a vet of the USA of where he spent twenty-four years serving the country and had $46,000 that he could use for mortgage. When I tried to use it, no company would give me a minute, much less a mortgage of twenty thousand to pay off my second mortgage. The deadline was on the twenty-fourth of December, and this required me to either do a short sale or find the money to pay the twenty thousand that was left on the second mortgage. One of my daughter's gave me ten thousand, but there was still ten thousand outstanding to be paid.

I knew that a way to my father's heart is through praise and worship.

It was early afternoon when I called a pastor for a word after feeling so distorted, but he was on the street heading home. I started to pray and question God about his conversation with Peter and reminded him how he told Peter to look in the fish mouth and take out money to pay taxes for them both. I heard a voice said, "Go to the casino!"

I said, "What!"

"Go to the casino."

This was not the first time I have been directed to use this means to get a blessing from God! This one was so big that I was wondering how was this going to work out. I continued to praise the Lord and go to the casino. While I was there, I heard, "Let's pray. Come on," and was listing to the prayer, and I was praying also! Let's pray was finished, and I was playing a worship song as I was sitting at a machine playing fifty cent.

A lot of people came and played the other machine beside me and showed me that they wanted the figure showing on the board that was two thousand and some one thousand, but I kept telling them that I only wanted the mega, which was thirteen thousand. I heard the song "Power Belongs to You," and I was singing when I saw people came running over to me and saying, "They gave it to you!"

I said, "What?"

"They give it to you," they said, "the mega."

I looked up, and the spin was on, and there it was, thirteen thousand! I jumped up and said, "Could you imagine the angel of the Lord boxed it out of their hands!"

The excitement came with a lot of people asking for things that I could not have given to them. One person was so precise of how much he wanted, and I said to him, "There is nothing here to give to you. You only see the mountain when it appears but you did not see the valley that I was in! God has just given me my mortgage." I got up and took the check and walked out!

# 39
## CHAPTER

*My beloved sister*

Friendship! Many times, we hear of this word. But do we really know its true meaning? What comes into mind when I think about it? Trust, love, sisterhood, joy, and the value of friendship, which is truly unmeasurable! I met my sister a few years back. She needed to get some work done, and it so happened that I was right there! Call it luck, but I think it was fate that brought us together. God had intended for us to meet that particular day—thanks to the internet. We started as strangers but developed into something beautiful—a bond that could never be broken! We ended up as the best of sisters.

My dear sister, you have taught me the meaning of true friendship, love, and sacrifice. I remember when you told me that you were coming down to Africa to see your niece, my daughter. We were so happy! You should have seen the look on her face when I told her about it. It was priceless! The memories created are dear to us. Your attitude and passion for the things of God are always something that I admire, that I have sought to achieve for myself. You have taught me so much since we met, and for that I am eternally grateful.

As I reflect on our friendship, my mind is filled with nothing but happy memories. Although you are miles away, it feels good to know that you will always be there to share my feelings, listen to me, and guide me as you have always been an inspiration and a role model. Thank you for being the best sister—so loving, caring, patient, understanding, kind, always willing to listen to me and to share your hopes and dreams with me. You are my sister, my hero, my role model, the best aunt ever. We love you with all our hearts, forever and always.

# 40
## CHAPTER

*A raven and dove assignment*

A person that is operating as a raven is one that is very intelligent, and yet they are the ones to do crazy scavenge. It is so revealing to me that people having beautiful homes who live with their own family are not satisfied. Some go out to work and come home with different agenda as one day they take a different route that leads them to a direction that diverts them to something that does not align with the assignment that they are assigned to. An example is a person who is looking for a job and walking through a door, and suddenly another person comes in, and they start a conversation that have nothing to do with the job that they are going for.

The conversation is carried out, and the job is not important anymore!

This leads that person to a different direction that I have noted for myself that someone close to me finds himself in such diversion that brings about changes in his home and disrupted his own home and mirage.

This changes the whole picture! This person's behavior is like a raven that is assigned to go out to look if there is dry land and does not return! We have these types sitting in the parks today, observing and seeking out people that they can scavenge from whether this person is a woman or a man.

As a raven waits for food, there are so many women or men that behave just like the ravens in their pursuit in relationship in their own homes. Some have a decent home, and yet they see someone passed them and say hi to them, and the end cannot be written. One scavenger woman picks up the wrong piece of meat that does not belons to her and have her own meat home but cannot be satisfied, and here comes trouble with this assignment.

> Remember them that are in bonds, as bound with them; and them which suffer adversity, as being yourselves also in the body. Marriage is honorable in all, and the bed undefiled: but whoremongers and adulterers God will judge. (Hebrews 13:3–4)

> Seek ye the Lord while he may be found, call ye upon him while he is near: Let the wicked forsake his way, and the unrighteous man his thoughts: and let him return unto the Lord, and he will have mercy upon him; and to our God, for he will abundantly pardon. For my thoughts are not your thoughts, neither are your ways my ways, saith the Lord. For as the heavens are higher than the earth, so are my ways higher than your ways, and my thoughts than your thoughts. For as the rain cometh down, and the snow from heaven, and returneth not thither, but watereth the earth, and maketh it bring forth and bud, that it may give seed to the sower, and bread to the eater: So shall my word be that goeth forth out of my mouth: it shall not return unto me void, but it shall accomplish that which I please, and it shall prosper in the thing whereto I sent it. For ye shall go out with joy, and be led forth with peace: the mountains and the hills shall break forth before you into singing, and all the trees of the field shall clap their hands. (Isaiah 55:6–12)

*Elijah predicts a drought*

> Now Elijah the Tishbite, of Tishbe in Gilead, said to Ahab, "As the Lord, the God of Israel, lives, before whom I stand, there shall be neither dew nor rain these years, except by my word." And the word of the Lord came to him: "Depart from here and turn eastward and hide yourself by the brook Cherith, which is east of the Jordan. You shall drink from the brook, and I have commanded the ravens to feed you there." So he went and did according to the word of the Lord. He went and lived by the brook Cherith that is east of the Jordan. And the ravens brought him bread and meat in the morning, and bread and meat in the evening, and he drank from the brook. And after a while the brook dried up, because there was no rain in the land. (1 Kings 17)

> Every word of God proves true; he is a shield to those who take refuge in him. Do not add to his words, lest he rebuke you and you be found a liar.
> Two things I ask of you; deny them not to me before I die: Remove far from me falsehood and lying; give me neither poverty nor riches; feed me with the food that is needful for me,
> lest I be full and deny you and say, "Who is the Lord?" or lest I be poor and steal and profane the name of my God. (Proverbs 30:5–9)

The first bird specifically mentioned in the Bible is the raven (Gen 8:6–7). While most people remember that Noah sent out a dove from the ark to find out if dry land was available for the rescued humans and animals after the flood, fewer recall that he first sent out a raven. The fact that the raven didn't return provided Noah with only part of the answer he was seeking: The bird had found some food to scavenge, but Noah still had no way to tell how much land was visible. The dove's thoughtful return with a branch gave the original ship captain confidence that the earth was returning to normal, but the dove hadn't found enough vegetation to survive on, and so it returned (Luke 12:24). Ravens are a particularly good symbol for God's providential care because they engage in a behavior called caching. They eat some food right away, but some they save in a particular spot and come back for later. And they are smart enough to remember where their caches are unlike some animals. While the raven is like Satan: not helping, not caring, not wanting to be saved, and looks forward to one's misfortunes.

The symbolic meaning of the raven in Native American Indian lore describes the raven as a creature of metamorphosis and symbolizes change/transformation. In some tribes, the raven is considered a trickster because of its transforming/changing attributes. Often honored among medicine and holy men of tribes for its shape-shifting qualities, the raven is called upon in ritual so that visions can be clarified. Native holy men understand that what the physical eye sees is not necessarily the truth, and he will call upon the raven for clarity in these matters. Foremost, the raven is the Native American bearer of magic and a harbinger of messages from the cosmos. Messages that are beyond space and time are nestled in the midnight wings of the raven and come to only those within the tribe who are worthy of the knowledge (https://www.symbolic-meanings.com/2007/11/15/symbolic-meaning-of-the-raven-in-native-american-indian-lore/).

Maybe we were not living as a dove before but as a raven and decided to walk away from a life of scavenger. Now we are living a life that glorified God!

> Therefore by the deeds of the law there shall
> no flesh be justified in his sight: for by the law is
> the knowledge of sin. But now the righteousness
> of God without the law is manifested, being wit-
> nessed by the law and the prophets; Even the righ-
> teousness of God which is by faith of Jesus Christ
> unto all and upon all them that believe: for there is

no difference: For all have sinned, and come short of the glory of God; Being justified freely by his grace through the redemption that is in Christ Jesus: Whom God hath set forth to be a propitiation through faith in his blood, to declare his righteousness for the remission of sins that are past, through the forbearance of God; To declare, I say, at this time his righteousness: that he might be just, and the justifier of him which believeth in Jesus. (Romans 3:23–26)

# 41
## CHAPTER

*A dove and their assignment*

As a dove, the world can be changing and everything turning upside down, but it is impossible to divert the dove from the assignment that God gave it!

I have become as a dove in my assignment now that I have lived like a raven a long time ago and know now that I am set in my assignment. There I have people who are set to try to divert me. But as a dove, I am focused on my call. I am in my spiritual position, and things are falling into place like never before in my entire life.

> But the dove found no place to rest her foot, and she returned to him in the ark, because water still covered the surface of all the earth. So he reached out his hand and brought her back inside the ark.
>
> And he stayed yet other seven days; and again he sent forth the dove out of the ark; And the dove came in to him in the evening; and, lo, in her mouth was an olive leaf pluckt off: so Noah knew that the waters were abated from off the earth. And he stayed yet other seven days; and sent forth the dove; which returned not again unto him anymore. (Genesis 8:9–12)

And he went into all the region around the Jordan, preaching a baptism of repentance for the remission of sins, as it is written in the book of the words of Isaiah the prophet, saying:

"The voice of one crying in the wilderness: 'Prepare the way of the Lord; Make His paths straight. Every valley shall be filled. And every mountain and hill brought low; The crooked places shall be made straight And the rough ways smooth; And all flesh shall see the salvation of God.'"

Maybe we were not living as a dove before, but as a Raven, and decided to walk away from a life of scavenger. (Luke 3:3–6)

Now as the people were in expectation, and all reasoned in their hearts about John, whether he was the Christ or not, John answered, saying to all, "I indeed baptize you with water; but One mightier than I is coming, whose sandal strap I am not worthy to loose. He will baptize you with the Holy Spirit and fire. His winnowing fan is in His hand, and He will thoroughly clean out His threshing floor, and gather the wheat into His barn; but the chaff He will burn with unquenchable fire." (Luke 3:15–17)

When all the people were baptized, it came to pass that Jesus also was baptized; and while He prayed, the heaven was opened. And the Holy Spirit descended in bodily form like a dove upon Him, and a voice came from heaven which said, "You are My beloved Son; in You I am well pleased." (Luke 3:21–22)

# 42
## CHAPTER

*Tears*

I have cried a million buckets of tears—some tears of joy, some tears of laughter, tears of shame, bad tears, good tears, and tears of sorrow, and many different types of tears throughout my little lifetime!

This morning, while I was in my restroom taking a shower and singing, I asked the Lord to give me an angel voice as a young lady that I heard sing in Europe! I was singing and forgotten all about what I asked the Lord for! Then I heard, "You can sing like an angel. But if you don't have love, you have nothing!"

Then I said, "Thank you, Lord, for what you have given to me."

There it went again another tears!

> If I speak in the tongues of men and of angels, but have not love, I am a noisy gong or a clanging cymbal. And if I have prophetic powers, and understand all mysteries and all knowledge, and if I have all faith, so as to remove mountains, but have not love, I am nothing. If I give away all I have, and if I deliver up my body to be burned, but have not love, I gain nothing. Love is patient and kind; love does not envy or boast; it is not arrogant or rude. It does not insist on its own way; it is not irritable or resentful; it does not rejoice at wrong-doing, but rejoices with the truth. Love bears all

things, believes all things, hopes all things, endures all things. Love never ends. As for prophecies, they will pass away; as for tongues, they will cease; as for knowledge, it will pass away. For we know in part and we prophesy in part, but when the perfect comes, the partial will pass away. When I was a child, I spoke like a child, I thought like a child, I reasoned like a child. When I became a man, I gave up childish ways. For now we see in a mirror dimly, but then face to face. Now I know in part; then I shall know fully, even as I have been fully known. So now faith, hope, and love abide, these three; but the greatest of these is love. (1 Corinthians 13:1–13)

But if there's anything in me that's not yet mature enough after all those tears, I would like someone who is a bold person to look for to wiped and flog my bottom so hard that I can cry another set of tears because I wouldn't have been great for the Lord who has been my shelter throughout all these tears!

You have kept count of my tossings; put my tears in your bottle. Are they not in your book? (Psalm 56:8)

He will wipe away every tear from their eyes, and death shall be no more, neither shall there be mourning, nor crying, nor pain anymore, for the former things have passed away. (Revelation 21:4)

My friends scorn me; my eye pours out tears to God. (Job 16:20)

Those who sow in tears shall reap with shouts of joy! (Psalm 126:5)

For the Lamb in the midst of the throne
will be their shepherd, and he will guide them to
springs of living water, and God will wipe away
every tear from their eyes." (Revelation 7:17)

The question is, is there anyone who has never cried some of
these tears? Well I'm persuaded that God's perfect will will soon manifest itself in your life, and you will never be the same again!

# 43
## CHAPTER

*Prayers of saints and the prayers of unbelievers—unanswered prayer*

You ask and do not receive, because you ask with wrong motives, so that you may spend it on your pleasures. (James 4:3)

If I regard wickedness in my heart,
The Lord will not hear. (Psalm 66:18)

But your iniquities have made a separation between you and your God,
And your sins have hidden His face from you so that He does not hear. (Isaiah 59:2, Source: https://bible.knowing-jesus.com/topics/Unanswered-Prayer)

Thou hast also given me the necks of mine enemies; that I might destroy them that hate me.
They cried, but there was none to save them: even unto the Lord, but he answered them not.
Then did I beat them small as the dust before the wind: I did cast them out as the dirt in the streets. (Psalm 18:40–42)

# 44
## CHAPTER

*Birds cannot fly on broken wings.*

W hen I realized that bird cannot fly with broken wings, I started to search myself to see the brokenness of my own life. From a child growing up, I would look at other people how they led their lives on different things that lead to brokenness and unaware of how it would affect their life further down the line. I must say that the thought of this makes me a lot stronger in God now!

Everything that was broken in my life is a pathway to all the miracles that God uses to hold me up during this brokenness to hold me up and take me from the beginning of a bad relationship to one with God where there is no creed or religions but one with God that I cannot regret now! Now even when we are at a crossroad in this life or imagining that it is in the life to come. My heart yearns for love that cannot be explained to any human being that has not gone through this type of unfairness in life as a child that did not know right from wrong but knew what love was!

As a child, no one uses the word love! Is love a bad word, or is it conveniently used as a bribe when people want to get the better part of you that is already compromised? There is no one there to wipe your tears at night. When things appear, when sleeping is hard from the nightmares, no one to read a book to, or tuck you in bed. There is nothing to reflect on that as an adult helps to tell you a joke that can bring out the laughter or giggles that help a child to rejuvenate from a long day away at school so that they can become themselves again!

How dare me to say that sometimes, the things that are hidden inside could be the key to navigate that brokenness of the hidden objects that need to let go of the pain.

When a father is missing out of a child's life, that is every young child's horror as a superhero is not there to protect them from harm or as a safety net to catch them from falling into hurtful things or from a mean person who prey on harmless people. When the realization kicks in that there is no one to speak to about what to expect from the opposite sex in life, it makes you feel that discomforting way of life that hits to the core! How can this be right? When others speak of the great relationship that they are experiencing in their own home circle, and that is only an imagination in your mind you are experiencing this moment knowing that it could be a lie. But God! When God found you—rather when you found God—you are safe, and you are secure in his arms!

Broken things are what God is specialized in fixing! I don't remember what it was like to be so broken in some areas of my life that I could not explain this to anyone that has not been through this type of unhappiness in life that makes you feel so fearful to even explain small things that would help you to help others with things that matters and to help others to then move onward. After a process has been taken place, it must begin with the first steps of heading in the right direction.

The word that came to Jeremiah from the Lord: "Arise, and go down to the potter's house, and there I will let you hear[a] my words." So I went down to the potter's house, and there he was working at his wheel. And the vessel he was making of clay was spoiled in the potter's hand, and he reworked it into another vessel, as it seemed good to the potter to do.

Then the word of the Lord came to me: "O house of Israel, can I not do with you as this potter has done? declares the Lord. Behold, like the clay in the potter's hand, so are you in my hand, O house of Israel. If at any time I declare concerning a nation or a kingdom, that I will pluck up and break down and destroy it. (Jeremiah 18:1–7)

He heals the brokenhearted, and binds up their wounds. He determines the number of the stars; he gives to all of them their names. Great is our Lord, and abundant in power; his understanding is beyond measure. (Psalm 147:3–5)

Knowing that the testing of your faith produces [a]patience. But let patience have its perfect work, that you may be [b]perfect and complete, lacking nothing. If any of you lacks wisdom, let him ask of God, who gives to all liberally and without reproach, and it will be given to him. But let him ask in faith, with no doubting, for he who doubts is like a wave of the sea driven and tossed by the wind. For let not that man suppose that he will receive anything from the Lord; He is a double-minded man, unstable in all his ways. (James 1:3–8)

# 45
## CHAPTER

*The fast that God choose*

For you will not delight in sacrifice, or I would give it; you will not be pleased with a burnt offering. The sacrifices of God are a broken spirit; a broken and contrite heart, O God, you will not despise. (Psalm 51:16–17)

Leave the way, turn aside from the path, let us hear no more about the Holy One of Israel." Therefore thus says the Holy One of Israel, "Because you despise this word and trust in oppression and perverseness and rely on them, therefore this iniquity shall be to you like a breach in a high wall, bulging out and about to collapse, whose breaking comes suddenly, in an instant; and its breaking is like that of a potter's vessel that is smashed so ruthlessly that among its fragments not a shard is found with which to take fire from the hearth, or to dip up water out of the cistern." For thus said the Lord God, the Holy One of Israel, "In returning and rest you shall be saved; in quietness and in trust shall be your strength." But you were unwilling, and you said, "No! We will flee upon horses"; therefore you shall flee away;

and, "We will ride upon swift steeds"; therefore your pursuers shall be swift. (Isaiah 30:11–16)

Wherefore have we fasted, say they, and thou seest not? wherefore have we afflicted our soul, and thou takest no knowledge? Behold, in the day of your fast ye find pleasure, and exact all your labours. Behold, ye fast for strife and debate, and to smite with the fist of wickedness: ye shall not fast as ye do this day, to make your voice to be heard on high. Is it such a fast that I have chosen? a day for a man to afflict his soul? is it to bow down his head as a bulrush, and to spread sackcloth and ashes under him? wilt thou call this a fast, and an acceptable day to the Lord? Is not this the fast that I have chosen? to loose the bands of wickedness, to undo the heavy burdens, and to let the oppressed go free, and that ye break every yoke? Is it not to deal thy bread to the hungry, and that thou bring the poor that are cast out to thy house? when thou seest the naked, that thou cover him; and that thou hide not thyself from thine own flesh? Then shall thy light break forth as the morning, and thine health shall spring forth speedily: and thy righteousness shall go before thee; the glory of the Lord shall be thy rereward. Then shalt thou call, and the Lord shall answer; thou shalt cry, and he shall say, Here I am. If thou take away from the midst of thee the yoke, the putting forth of the finger, and speaking vanity; And if thou draw out thy soul to the hungry, and satisfy the afflicted soul; then shall thy light rise in obscurity, and thy darkness be as the noonday.

And the Lord of hosts shall stir up a scourge for him according to the slaughter of Midian at the rock of Oreb: and as his rod was upon the sea, so shall he lift it up after the manner of Egypt.

And it shall come to pass in that day, that his burden shall be taken away from off thy shoulder, and his yoke from off thy neck, and the yoke shall be destroyed because of the anointing. (Isaiah 58)

# 46
## CHAPTER

*The sides*

There are two sides in life. Some people say there are three!
I know that there is a right side and a left side. When God said not to turn to the right or the left side, that's how I know that it's only two sides. Every coin has two sides. I am a stable person until someone gives me a reason to be unstable!

I am at work all week, and the work is not hard. So I'm doing my best to continue to work with no problems. But at the end of the week, when I am getting everything in order to leave work half hour before that time, here comes the crazy stuff that starts to manifest itself, trying to manipulate me, thinking that this will ever work in my life!

My telephone starts ringing call after call, and everyone automatically has something to talk about that's important suddenly! I don't know if people only think that, in life, they are the only ones that have another side!

> Then Moses stood in the gate of the camp,
> and said, Who is on the Lord's side? let him come
> unto me. And all the sons of Levi gathered them-
> selves together unto him. And he said unto them,
> Thus saith the Lord God of Israel, Put every man
> his sword by his side, and go in and out from gate
> to gate throughout the camp, and slay every man

his brother, and every man his companion, and
every man his neighbour. (Exodus 32:26)

Well I was tested this week to show that I have another side also!
So I refused to be a runover by others. As I left my report and the
phone calls kept coming in, I decided to take a stand and let them
know that I wouldn't be talking to anyone when I am about to leave
work, and about anything pertaining to work when I am away from
work; but for some reason, they didn't get the memo!

My telephone kept ringing, and texts kept coming, but it had no
bearing on me because I was finished with work one hour ago!

The next day, a text was coming in from work, but I didn't even
look at it until I got back to work because I am entitled to my weekend
off! Is London bridge on fire burning down? I came in to work, and
everything remained the same!

I opened the text after one hour when I was settled in at work, and
there was no alarm because it was for bloodwork. It was Tuesday—not
morning nor afternoon. They didn't mention when. Today was only
Monday! What was the emergency again?

No evil will befall you nor any plague come near your dwelling!

> A thousand may fall at your side,
> ten thousand at your right hand,
> but it will not come near you.
> You will only observe with your eyes
> and see the punishment of the wicked.
> If you say, "The Lord is my refuge,"
> and you make the Most High your dwelling,
> no harm will overtake you,
> no disaster will come near your tent.
> For he will command his angels concerning you
> to guard you in all your ways. (Psalm 91)

Solomon instructed his son not to turn aside from the Lord to
the right or to the left.

He was the wisest man who ever lived, so he knew about life. He had explored it from the center and both sides (Ecclesiastes 1:2–2:26). He recognized that the right and the left were futility and vexation of spirit. At the end, he pled with anyone who would listen not to turn aside from the Lord to the right or to the left.

> Therefore be ye very courageous to keep and to do all that is written in the book of the law of Moses, that ye turn not aside therefrom to the right hand or to the left. (Joshua 23:6)

I thank Lord God that you are the only true and dreadful God; yet you are the only loving and merciful God, and there is no one like you!

> Again I say unto you, that if two of you shall agree on earth as touching anything that they shall ask, it shall be done for them of my Father which is in heaven. (Matthew 18:19)

Satan's plan was to get the attention of the woman. When God made man it was for us to live in the Garden of Eden, and never be in wanted for anything at all. When Satan sees the plan of God; as he was the highest angel in heaven that sing and minister to God! He expired his time when he became very envious of the blessing of God. He Satan started to think on how he could have what God has! I could imagine how he sits down days after day and night after nights to hash a plan to see if he can dethrone God.

The Bible tells us that he has no intention of stopping even now. He tries everything that attach to the promise of God. Satan goes to and fro from heaven to earth to see if he could accuse us daily. When he was thrown out of heaven he started a campaign that was just the beginning of the plan he had in mind, because he his very intelligent. Do you want to know how intelligent Satan is?

Check the way how he tempt Jesus when he went and followed Jesus after his fasting on the mountain.

At that time Jesus was led by the Spirit into the desert to be tempted by the devil. He fasted for forty days and forty nights and afterwards was hungry. The tempter approached and said to him, "If you are the Son of God, command that these stones become loaves of bread. Jesus answered, "It is written: 'Man shall not live on bread alone, but on every word that comes from the mouth of God.'[b]"

Then the devil took him to the holy city and had him stand on the highest point of the temple. "If you are the Son of God," he said, "throw yourself down. For it is written:

"'He will command his angels concerning you,

and they will lift you up in their hands,

so that you will not strike your foot against a stone.'"

Jesus answered him, "It is also written: 'Do not put the Lord your God to the test.'"

Again, the devil took him to a very high mountain and showed him all the kingdoms of the world and their splendor. "All this I will give you," he said, "if you will bow down and worship me." (Matthew 4:1–11)

Don't loose sight of where you are going! When Satan sees that he couldn't get Jesus attention he started to strategize how to get someone's attention.

He was hiding in the Garden of Eden somewhere plotting to see what he could use.

# 47

## CHAPTER

*Judas walked*

He was one of the twelve disciples that Jesus chose; and yet walking with Jesus, he was not a good person that was godly. The heart is desperately wicked about all!

As they were reclining at the table and eating, Jesus said, "Truly I say to you that one of you will betray Me—one who is eating with Me." (Mark 14:18)

When Jesus had said this, He became troubled in spirit, and testified and said, "Truly, truly, I say to you, that one of you will betray Me." (John 13:21)

Peter, turning around, *saw the disciple whom Jesus loved following them; the one who also had leaned back on His bosom at the supper and said, "Lord, who is the one who betrays You?" (John 21:20)

But there are some of you who do not believe." For Jesus knew from the beginning who

they were who did not believe, and who it was that
would betray him. (John 6:64)

Judas went on a mission to betray Jesus in a way that no one
could ever imagine! Eating and praying daily with Jesus, but his heart
was at thirty pieces of silver away! This shows us that even though
Judas was walking with Jesus, he was not aligned with the blessing that
Jesus was giving out freely. They were not in one accord as they were
not agreeing.

*He hung himself*

> Then Judas, His betrayer, seeing that He had
> been condemned, was remorseful and brought
> back the thirty pieces of silver to the chief priests
> and elders, saying, "I have sinned by betraying
> innocent blood." And they said, "What is that to
> us? You see to it!" Then he threw down the pieces
> of silver in the temple and departed, and went and
> hanged himself. (Matthew 27:3–5)

The word of God said that God's ways are not our ways, and
God's thoughts are not our thoughts.

> "For my thoughts are not your thoughts, nei-
> ther are your ways my ways," declares the Lord.
> "As the heavens are higher than the earth,
> so are my ways higher than your ways and my
> thoughts than your thoughts. (Isaiah 55:8–9)

Alas, he saw Adam and Eve and he got what he was looking for!
Satan's not of God. He is a liar from the beginning. In the Bible, he was
described as the father of lies.

> You belong to your father, the devil, and you
> want to carry out your father's desires. He was a

murderer from the beginning, not holding to the truth, for there is no truth in him. When he lies, he speaks his native language, for he is a liar and the father of lies. (John 8:44)

He saw a serpent, and he used the serpent's body to do his deeds as the Bible tells us that the servant was very intelligent about all the wild animals that God made. He approached Eve in the Garden of Eden and started a conversation. The devil is looking for your attention, and he gets the point across that he just wants one minute of your time. Satan didn't approach Adam because he knew that Adam was set aside to answer only to God! Satan questioned Eve about the conversation that they had with God and what God advised them not to do. Then he said, "I will tell you that the minute you do what God says not to, you will become like God!" This one minute, Satan slithered away, knowing that he got his one minute of her attention!

Now the serpent was more subtil than any beast of the field which the Lord God had made. And he said unto the woman, Yea, hath God said, Ye shall not eat of every tree of the garden? And the woman said unto the serpent, We may eat of the fruit of the trees of the garden: But of the fruit of the tree which is in the midst of the garden, God hath said, Ye shall not eat of it, neither shall ye touch it, lest ye die. And the serpent said unto the woman, Ye shall not surely die: For God doth know that in the day ye eat thereof, then your eyes shall be opened, and ye shall be as gods, knowing good and evil. And when the woman saw that the tree was good for food, and that it was pleasant to the eyes, and a tree to be desired to make one wise, she took of the fruit thereof, and did eat, and gave also unto her husband with her; and he did eat. And the eyes of them both were opened, and they knew that they were naked; and they sewed

fig leaves together, and made themselves aprons.
(Genesis 3)

And unto Adam he said, Because thou hast
hearkened unto the voice of thy wife, and hast
eaten of the tree, of which I commanded thee, saying, Thou shalt not eat of it: cursed is the ground
for thy sake; in sorrow shalt thou eat of it all the
days of thy life. (Genesis 3)

# 48

## CHAPTER

*Special piece written by my baby daughter*

She was only a young girl from a small community in Jamaica. Her journey started in 2015 when she graduated from high school in Jamaica then took her SATs. They were not very common in Jamaica, so it was very expensive to pay for in that time where she lived. Despite the price, classes were paid and were the best means of information she could have to move forward!

As a child growing up, I was taught to be satisfied with the simple things in life, and that was my goal—to be simple. Leaving all the other things behind was a challenge, but when I started to attend college in the United States, I just grasped it with a passion. I started helping people to move into the direction that they love. In 2016, arriving in the Big Apple, as they call New York, this was the hardest goal one could ever start without knowing the root of what college for the fall semester would ever bring.

Everything went well until she received an email from the college that she was chosen as more light shone on the way to inform her that a Jamaican transcript was not going to be accepted, and more issues arose as evaluation process was near. At that moment, it felt like an extra weight had been laid on her shoulder. This would cause anyone in this position to want to give up. But she knew that everything in life had consequences, and that was not what the plan of God had in store for her.

After waiting and praying, things turned around. After all documents were reevaluated, starting in the spring semester of 2017 was the best choice. I practiced the thoughts of speaking positive things when it came to the goals beforehand and kept what should be considered a big issue by the administration at the college a mere glitch. They kept holding back the information that was the backbone of the processing of the financial aid documents and personal information that were not added to the process until shortly after. It is written in the Bible:

> The mouth of the righteous speaketh wisdom, and his tongue talketh of judgment.
> The law of his God is in his heart; none of his steps shall slide.
> The wicked watcheth the righteous, and seeketh to slay him.
> The Lord will not leave him in his hand, nor condemn him when he is judged.
> Wait on the Lord, and keep his way, and he shall exalt thee to inherit the land: when the wicked are cut off, thou shalt see it.
> I have seen the wicked in great power, and spreading himself like a green bay tree.
> Yet he passed away, and, lo, he was not: yea, I sought him, but he could not be found.
> Mark the perfect man, and behold the upright: for the end of that man is peace.
> But the transgressors shall be destroyed together: the end of the wicked shall be cut off.
> But the salvation of the righteous is of the Lord: he is their strength in the time of trouble.
> Approaching a major in Nursing was the goal, then courses were difficult so switching was a better choice to occupational therapy, and then it came down to a bottle between the two and Health Sciences prevail! (Psalm)

A double minded man is unstable in all his
ways. (James 1:8)

That making of this decision became clear that there was no time
to change for another major. In the year of 2021, completing a bache-
lor's degree in health sciences set a milestone for starting out late. But
she finished quickly at a young age of twenty-two. After such short
time, a pat on the back was well due! I can do all things through Christ
which strengths me!

God works in mysterious ways. After facing all those obstacles,
I think that if giving up was an option, the thought never would have
worked because giving up would be the last resort! Because of those
ups and downs, there would not have been any silver lining over the
dark clouds after pursuing something that helped to remodel the goal
of helping others agreed with the direction set before us! Following the
path that was set out for nursing or occupational therapy was not the
right decision, and it helped with the way it landed on other's lap with
refinement, and that's what counts—managing to help people in other
ways that count immensely always!

# 49
## CHAPTER

*Before the jump*

It was all he could think about being airborne. Tom spent twenty-four years in the American Army and thought it was a great way to get the promotion to move forward to a higher-ranking level as he starved for the wings medal pin that enticed him to want to jump so badly. He approached everything in life with a passion that seemed like this was not real! He said, "At first I agreed to do airborne because I thought it was the best thing ever as it looked so good from afar that I can get the wings medal to put in my collection of pins. I joined the group of jumpers, and we boarded the aircraft as they started testing, and then I realized I was not thinking right. Let me ask you a question! Why would anyone want to jump out of a perfectly good plane? You see, this is why I am changing my mind!"

*Elisha with Elijah—Elijah taken up to heaven*

> When the Lord was about to take Elijah up to heaven in a whirlwind, Elijah and Elisha were on their way from Gilgal. Elijah said to Elisha, "Stay here; the Lord has sent me to Bethel."
> But Elisha said, "As surely as the Lord lives and as you live, I will not leave you." So they went down to Bethel.

The company of the prophets at Bethel came out to Elisha and asked, "Do you know that the Lord is going to take your master from you today?"

"Yes, I know," Elisha replied, "so be quiet."

Then Elijah said to him, "Stay here, Elisha; the Lord has sent me to Jericho."

And he replied, "As surely as the Lord lives and as you live, I will not leave you." So they went to Jericho.

The company of the prophets at Jericho went up to Elisha and asked him, "Do you know that the Lord is going to take your master from you today?"

"Yes, I know," he replied, "so be quiet."

Then Elijah said to him, "Stay here; the Lord has sent me to the Jordan."

And he replied, "As surely as the Lord lives and as you live, I will not leave you." So the two of them walked on.

Fifty men from the company of the prophets went and stood at a distance, facing the place where Elijah and Elisha had stopped at the Jordan. Elijah took his cloak, rolled it up and struck the water with it. The water divided to the right and to the left, and the two of them crossed over on dry ground.

When they had crossed, Elijah said to Elisha, "Tell me, what can I do for you before I am taken from you?"

As they were walking along and talking together, suddenly a chariot of fire and horses of fire appeared and separated the two of them, and Elijah went up to heaven in a whirlwind. Elisha saw this and cried out, "My father! My father! The chariots and horsemen of Israel!" And Elisha saw him no more. Then he took hold of his garment and tore it in two.

Elisha then picked up Elijah's cloak that had fallen from him and went back and stood on the bank of the Jordan. He took the cloak that had fallen from Elijah and struck the water with it. "Where now is the Lord, the God of Elijah?" he asked. When he struck the water, it divided to the right and to the left, and he crossed over.

The company of the prophets from Jericho, who were watching, said, "The spirit of Elijah is resting on Elisha." And they went to meet him and bowed to the ground before him. "Look," they said, "we your servants have fifty able men. Let them go and look for your master. Perhaps the Spirit of the Lord has picked him up and set him down on some mountain or in some valley."

"No," Elisha replied, "do not send them."

But they persisted until he was too embarrassed to refuse. So he said, "Send them." And they sent fifty men, who searched for three days but did not find him. When they returned to Elisha, who was staying in Jericho, he said to them, "Didn't I tell you not to go?" (2 Kings 2)

Knowing that Elijah assignment was in full progression with God as Elisa knew that one day he will taste the goodness of God! Every where Elijah goes Elisha follows, because there is something he wants so bad he could touch it...

# 50
## CHAPTER

*Conclusion*

I took the word of GOD seriously as that was given to me from all prophets years ago!

God has spoken once. Twice have I heard this that power belongs to God!

When God reminded me about the spoken word from his prophet from years ago, I became alive again as his words are in my life. I have experienced gunshots all around my home, even when I was shouting duck, baby, duck, and it didn't affect me or my property!

The expectation of the wicked will not be met in my life.

> Ye shall not fear them: for the Lord your
> God he shall fight for you. (Deuteronomy 3:22)

The word of God is a consuming fire. And on my tree, the fire burns in degrees—first, second and third degrees!

The problem is not that I was not giving in God's ministries but because I was not consulting God.

I learned to depend on God. I am grateful for the gift of God. As nature presents itself, I choose right from wrong. And then I smelled that the water was dried up out of the pot with the eggs I was not flustered. I said, "Oh Lord God, how can someone burn eggs! I just did."

And we know that all things work together
for good to them that love God, to them who are
called according to his purpose. (Romans 8:28)

Fruit baskets are full with different types of fruits and vegetables.

No good trees bear bad fruits, nor does a bad
tree bears good fruit. (Luke 6:43)

A father is the monarch of the house of God and teaches his children the truth and steer them into the right direction!

As I was prophesying, things were coming together. The delicious plate of wickedness was devoured, and I still stand to speak about it! Not everyone can fit in my shoes as the discomfort of it will make them surrender.

Don't let me pray. As I started to pray there was silence after a while; then the line went dead!

After learning to walk in obedience and started to focus on my walk with God, things became very easy, not smooth, because there were levels and levels! Trouble is always attached to people who try to get away from trouble but attract trouble by adaption!

Yet man that is born unto trouble, as the
sparks fly upward. (Job 5:7)

It is evident from the analysis of the pros and cons of insecurity that psychological insecurity is directly correlated to mental illnesses, such as anxiety, narcissism, paranoid personality, and depression. Insecurity also triggers depression due to feelings of low self-worth and a lack of sense of belonging. People with low self-worth are more likely to concentrate on and magnify their shortcomings, thus feeding on insecurity.

It is important to embrace positive emotions as a way of avoiding the cons related to psychological insecurity. Eliminating lack of confidence based on social anxiety starts by talking to your inner critic. Self-reflection will enable you to remind yourself about your shortcomings particularly during social interactions. This will allow you to understand your weaknesses and strengths in social interactions, hence improving your sense of belonging. I learned that even when I am having trouble interacting with others, I should encourage myself not to avoid social gatherings. Back then, even when I was feeling uncomfortable or nervous, I still attended social events.

> But when you ask, you must believe and not doubt, because the one who doubts is like a wave of the sea, blown and tossed by the wind. (James 1:6)

This decreased my social anxiety eventually and stimulated my self-worth, thereby decreasing the insecurity. Furthermore, I deliberately focused on others in order to combat intense self-focus. This is essential in enhancing your self-awareness. As such, practicing positive emotions would eliminate insecurity by helping you improve your self-awareness, self-worth, and sense of belonging while interacting socially.

> There is no fear in love, but perfect love casts out fear. For fear has to do with punishment, and whoever fears has not been perfected in love. (1 John 4:18)

Insecurity and how it impacts your life has pros and cons as well as everything in life! Ravens' and doves' assignments are not the same as they are heading into different directions!

Tears are reserved for special times when it's ready to flow in every area of your life.

Birds cannot fly with broken wings as the wings need to expand and stretch out as the wind passes through and gives it the push it needs to fly! God's ways are not man's nor God's thoughts are man's thoughts. As the heavens are higher than the earth, so is God!

Again I say unto you, that if two of you shall agree on earth as touching anything that they shall ask, it shall be done for them of my Father which is in heaven. (Matthew 18:19)

# ABOUT THE AUTHOR

She is known as a prayer warrior who receives answers from God! She is a minister of the Gospel of Christ for a number of years. Christianity was a part of her life as long as she could remember. Having a relationship with God is what makes the difference today in Joan Parris's life after spending time praying for others as one of the recent graduates of the first prophetic training school that was open this year 2021 in Paris, France, by Pastor Alph Lukau. Joan Parris has written *To Belong: My Seed in the Ground Speaks Louder than Any Enemy's Voice*, her first book that was published in the ending part of 2021 and completed a copy-written song that the Lord has inspired her with after a drastic episode of losing her breath—breath of God! Joan Parris is a family-orientated person. She spends more time with her family and loved ones. She is also called God Squad by her spouse. She spends time praying with people who call and tell her explicitly that the Lord instructed them to call her for prayer, or sometimes she calls someone, and the Holy Spirit takes over; and the prayer continues with tongues until the prayer is ended. Joan Parris tries her best to pray in the area according to what the Lord says.

Joan Parris used to go around adapting people's children, not changing their names or habitations but only giving to their lives and giving them a better way that they can live comfortably. But as the

COVID continues to be troubling in many countries, it makes me feel saddened by the effects that are presently suppressed by the way everything is being handled now.

Joan Parris lives her life on the foundation of the Word of God! Lots of miracles are happening daily now in people's lives, and those who prayed with her get their prayers answered. God is answering prayers now more than ever with evidence! They have tasted God's goodness and are awakened by new miracles every day from God!